"Me Laala"

Eulalia Ilene McCamly

WESTBOW
PRESS®
A DIVISION OF THOMAS NELSON
& ZONDERVAN

Copyright © 2022 Eulalia Ilene McCamly.

All rights reserved. No part of this book may be used or reproduced by any means, graphic, electronic, or mechanical, including photocopying, recording, taping or by any information storage retrieval system without the written permission of the author except in the case of brief quotations embodied in critical articles and reviews.

This book is a work of non-fiction. Unless otherwise noted, the author and the publisher make no explicit guarantees as to the accuracy of the information contained in this book and in some cases, names of people and places have been altered to protect their privacy.

WestBow Press books may be ordered through booksellers or by contacting:

WestBow Press
A Division of Thomas Nelson & Zondervan
1663 Liberty Drive
Bloomington, IN 47403
www.westbowpress.com
844-714-3454

Because of the dynamic nature of the Internet, any web addresses or links contained in this book may have changed since publication and may no longer be valid. The views expressed in this work are solely those of the author and do not necessarily reflect the views of the publisher, and the publisher hereby disclaims any responsibility for them.

Any people depicted in stock imagery provided by Getty Images are models, and such images are being used for illustrative purposes only. Certain stock imagery © Getty Images.

ISBN: 978-1-6642-5483-1 (sc)
ISBN: 978-1-6642-5484-8 (hc)
ISBN: 978-1-6642-5482-4 (e)

Library of Congress Control Number: 2022900934

Print information available on the last page.

WestBow Press rev. date: 01/20/2022

DEDICATION

This life story, not ended, is dedicated to my family
with all my love …

EULALIA ILENE MCCAMLY
January 2, 2022

PREFACE

One night I decided there were quite a lot of instances we weren't prepared to handle but to do nothing was not the way life should be. So, I began to write about life's happenings and a long life was ahead of me. God has ruled my being here. It was live and learn along the way. If one tries hard enough, they can accomplish hard trials in life and feel proud they did. What was so strange in what influenced me to put my life story in a book? I wanted to remind people how fortunate they are now with so many discoveries to make life easier. So few go through the hardships of the people from the "Old Country" as it was called and still called. Times were worse but people lived through it all and came out of it better people. Friends and neighbors helped each other. Now you hardly know your neighbor. They are self-centered. Care not what others say or do. We should wake up and take care of each other. I have lived so many years, beyond what I expected. I apologize for repeating parts of the stories throughout this book, but then again, I am up there in my years!

HERITAGE

Eulalia's great, great grandparents, on her mother's side of the family, were poor farmers coming over on a ship, which took months and months on the ocean. One day, Papa Hans said, "Regnheld, I believe we should sell all of our possessions and start preparing to take one of the few ships sailing to America."

"Ouch Hans", replied Regnheld, "that is such a journey. What will we do when we reach land? We can't eat dirt."

Hans replied, "but Regina", as she was called, "we have knives and guns to supply ourselves with food. With the fur and hides we can make coats, boots, and more. I'm sure there are small supply houses where we can purchase flour and seeds to plant. We won't leave our home here until we have plenty of dried foods to take and plenty of silver and gold to keep you and our children from starving. Many people are going to the New Country. The sooner we can go the better, before all the land is taken. I hear the country is very big and life is good."

So Regina started drying grains and foods that they could store in woven containers and did not take up too much room. Cloth was woven and clothing made. She made pouches of leather to wrap dishes and utensils in. Hans and Regina had a passel of children. There were Nels, Hans Jr., Regna, Bertha, Martha, and Gina. All little blonds only a year or so apart. There were still so many things to prepare for the journey. Hans worked not only his own land but assisted the neighbors for whatever dollar he could earn. The children who were old enough to go to school earned money helping neighbors with chores before school time. There were good hardworking children.

Soon it was winter again, and oh so cold. There were snow banks to climb to get to school and to town. The two boys were the oldest, so naturally they had to help get in the wood, milk the cows, feed the chickens, and gather eggs. The girls tried to help by letting Mother spend time at the spinning wheel while they cooked and washed dishes.

Everything was beginning to look dismal. Time was going by fast. Then Bertha seemed to be ailing in health. She ran a fever often, had bad coughs, and colds at least once a month. She became very pale and cried a lot. The old country doctor was summoned on a stormy, cold night. But the good old doc put on his fur cap and coat and hitched up his horse to the small buggy with runners on it to slide over the snow. He came around three o'clock in the morning. Low and behold, he found Bertha to have the whooping cough. Of course, all the children would catch it from her.

So Hans went to town to get some lamp oil, called kerosene, and with a few drops on a teaspoon of sugar, they could silence the cough. Finally, everyone got some sleep. Bertha survived the winter and come spring, she spent many hours out in the sunshine. In a month she was well again.

For three years they planned the big move. And the time finally came. Being as it would take so long to cross the ocean, they tried to travel during the warmer season. If there were no problems, they would reach America before the coldest part of the year. At the time of traveling to the New Country, America, they had Nels, Regna, Gina, and Hans, Jr.

Chapter 2: The Journey to the New Country, America

The journey on the ocean was almost unbearable. All became very sea sick and laid in their bunks for hours when the ocean was ragging a battle with the wind. One night, the wind blew them around like a piece of paper. Water was splashing into the ship, and the boys had to help bail water out. Regina and the girls had to get everything up as high as possible. There were other families on the ship too. There were also mischievous acts going on the deviltry.

Most of the boys were afraid of the captain. His beard was long and he clipped his hair off at the shoulders. He wore a halter to hold his saber and knives. This was because of sea pirates. He had fought and won numerous battles.

Preparing food on the ship was a skill tried by all the women and girls. Once a week they joined together their food and cooking supplies. Everyone had a good time singing and dancing.

A gala time was being had when the sky opened with thunder clapping and lightning to blind them. Rain came in torrents. The sails were nearly ripped to shreds. Smallest children cried and screamed with fear. One man fell over board.

Hans volunteered to try and rescue him, but the captain forbade it. "No Hans, you cannot. You have a wife and four hungry mouths to feed and raise." So that was settled in a hurry. Although Hans always felt guilty about the poor man's death.

They sailed and sailed. One morning the captain called out on his bullhorn that there was land ahead. The navigator said it was not America. The captain was only joking. It still took several days to reach the docks of New York City.

Chapter 3: Early Life in Oneida, New York

There was a station house for the immigrants to stay for a night. Then they were expected to go to an inn. There was a government office where they could get knowledge of land grants in every settled state in the United States. Oneida, New York, was Indian Territory, although they were quite civilized and gave the newcomers corn to plant and grind into meal.

They bought a covered wagon and a team of mules. Supplies were purchased to start to build their house. Hans wasn't much of a carpenter, but a shelter was put up for the family. Regina made straw mattresses from the neighbor's straw pile, so they wouldn't be sleeping on dry, dirty, cold sod.

Many of the neighbors gave them some essentials for inside the shelter. Hans made a table and benches for dining. The crude furnishings made it livable but not easy to clean. Hans bought a cow heavy with calf. She gave only a small amount of milk and butter. It was enough for the family to exist on, along with game and fish Hans killed for food, fur, and leather.

The school for the children was two miles away and they had to walk to and from until the snow got too deep. When the snow was too deep, Hans made runners with a platform on it and hitched up one of the mules.

He planted corn, wheat, and oats in the spring, working the soil with one mule hitched to a plow, which made one furrow at a time. Some of their grassland was rented to the neighbors for their horses and cattle to thrive on. In return, one rancher gave Hans a pair of working horses and one to ride. He was given three head of cattle from another man. One was for butchering for food the other two would start a herd. A couple of pigs were purchased and twelve laying hens. They felt very fortunate to have such wonderful neighbors, although they could hardly understand English or speak it very well.

Chapter 4: Moving West to Dakota Territory

The times had changed. The Hans family needed to expand their land and become the older settlers farther west. Once again, they started to prepare for a long trip across country. As they came to crossing rivers, they built rafts to carry their wagons, horses, and a couple of cows. They had sold the cattle and mules. Everything they could get along without, they sold. As they migrated west, they found small towns had been established. They could get provisions to make life easier for all.

They journeyed about thirty miles a day, so by the time winter hit again they were in Dakota Territory. Again, the government was granting land to settlers, and with money from the land sale in New

York, they were able to hire help to build a nice sized house. They were quite a few miles from a town called Eales and to the north of one called Akaska.

The Family Grows

Regna, the older of the girls, got a job as a schoolteacher. She had studied reading, writing, and arithmetic and was very good with the younger students. It was while she was teaching the Anderson children when she met and married Olaf, who was from Sweden. From their union, three children were born, Ruby, Otto, and Arthor. Ruby became a schoolteacher. Otto was not too young anymore by the time he married Jeanitto. To this union, one child was born. Arthor married later in life to Gloria. They had four children. Nels married a lady by the name of Anna. The men had established farms by then. Nels and Anna had one daughter, Ruth, and sons Alfred, Melvin, Haakon, and Edward.

Gina married Herman Rudd. I believe he was from Denmark. To this union Fred, Hans, Harold, Hilda, Mabel, and Bessie were born. For many years they remained in Potter County, South Dakota. Fred and Agnes had no children. Hans and Mabel raised four children. The women were sisters and, both families moved to Puyallup, Washington. Harold stayed a farmer in Potter County, South Dakota and raised a family of five girls and three boys.

Bertha married Frank Koep, a shyster of a businessman. They had this huge house in Gettysburg. Bertha took in boarders after Frank died at a young age. They had no children, but she kept a beautiful home, neat as a pin. And she was a good seamstress too.

Martha married Gilbert Johnson, who had come from the old country, Norway. They lived on the farm my great grandparents built and made a fair to good living. The great grandparents were buried in a cemetery called The Fayette Township Cemetery. Martha and Gilbert Johnson were hard working people and Martha rarely went to town. Gilbert went to town, which was twenty miles by team and wagon. He would be gone a few days. When he came home, the horses brought him as Gilbert was drunk as a skunk in the back of the wagon. Whenever possible my Aunt Nellie would find Gilbert's whiskey jug and break it on the wagon wheel. She would say she dropped it to keep from getting whipped.

Hans and Anna were born in Norway and came over on a ship. Anna married Herman Lenz and raised three sons. Each went into a different type of work. None wanted to be farmers. Hans married Elizabeth Leer and they had Erwin, Rapheal, and Elsie. Erwin and Rapheal married farmers' daughters, but Elsie was accidentally shot in a hunting accident at the age of sixteen. It was very tragic. John, called "Jack", married Anna White. Two children, Ray and Mildred, were born and after ten years they were divorced. Mildred lived with her mother and stepfather. Ray remained with his father until his stepmother, Susie, became so mean to him he chose to live with his uncle Ralph and Aunt Edith. Jack and Susie had a daughter, Myrtle, and a son Joyee. They also raised a granddaughter, Mary Jane.

Ralph married Edith Lemler. They had a son, Howard, who was killed in an auto accident. They had two daughters, Marla and Linda. Nellie, my favorite Aunt, married a Swede, Albert Larson. They were both so neat. I wanted to live with them as they had no children, but Mom and Dad wouldn't let me. I only visited a week or two at a time.

My mom, Eva, correct name Evaline, married my dad, Alvin Bartels on January 17, 1918. I will tell what I know about my dad's family after I finish with Mom's. Mom was 17 at the time of their marriage. My brother, Walter, was born December 8, 1918. He married Minnie Paulson and they raised six children. Dorthy married James Wilcox and they had six children, losing one to cancer in 1999. I married David on April 19, 1940. We were poor farmers for twenty-two years. We have five children living and a son who only lived for eleven hours. We sold our farm and traveled for six weeks.

Before I continue with my life, I'll tell you about my father's family. Both Grandma and Grandpa Bartels, Henrick and Doris, came from Germany but met and married in America.

My father's family is not large. Grandma Bartels, maiden name Nels Doris Paul, came from Germany with her aunt and uncle John

Pahl. They had no children at the time. All John's children were born in the United States. They were Helen Pahl Force-Louis, Fred, Charlie, and Adolph. Helen married Carl Force and moved to Indiana. One son and two daughters were born there and I only saw them once. Louise and Gladys had one son, who died from a heart attack in the 1990's. He came to them late in life and was an only child. Fred and Mary had a son, Dean and a daughter, Bonnie. Dean did very well as a rancher and then president of a bank. They had four sons. Bonnie married and moved to Colorado. The last time I saw Bonnie she was blind from diabetes and passed away at the age of sixty. Dean had a fatal heart attack at the age of sixty-five. Charlie, whom we all called "Big Charlie" married Hazel Plumber. A wonderful cook who ran a cafe in Mobridge, South Dakota for years after their family were all married and gone. Son, Donnie and daughter, Shirley live in Minnesota, around Minneapolis too. Adolph was married to Ruth and had one son, Bobby. Ruth passed away quite young. Adolph moved to North Dakota and remarried. I hadn't seen him in so many years. He never came back to South Dakota. Now, Grandma Doris Pahl, homesteaded on a section of land 320 acres. The government gave people land and some livestock to help make a living. Grandpa Bartels also came from Germany and migrated to Dakota Territory. He met Grandma and they were married. Grandpa being a carpenter, started adding rooms onto Grandma's one room shack. The house ended up to be three stories, 15 rooms, no basement. He built 12 buildings through the years on the land. Uncle Louie, whom we never met, was killed as a teenager on a horse. He was drug to death because his foot got caught in the stirrups. He was the oldest.

Uncle Willie was second born. He married Elsie Buckhalz and they had no children. Uncle Willie was not well and passed away in his forties after having gotten the home place in deep debt.

Aunt Elsa married William Packard. They were both such neat people. They had three boys and one girl.

My cousin Bob was killed in a truck accident. The truck caught on fire and he and his company driver both burned to ashes. No one knows for sure who was driving at the time. Edward and Roger are still living. Doris passed away from cancer in 1972. She had three boys, all grown, married, and living in different parts of the country. Edward and Thelma have one daughter. Marleen and Roger had one son, Scott, from his first marriage.

My dad, Alvin, was also born in the same farm house. He was a math whiz. He went to Austin, Minnesota to business college for a while but ended up married and a farmer for the many years he and Mom were married. They were married for forty-nine years until his death in 1967. I had a brother Walter, sister Dorthy, then came me, then Mary Ruth and last, Martha Luann, who got pneumonia and whooping cough. Martha Luann lived only 28 days. We other four kids had the whooping cough when Martha Luann was born and of course she was born at home.

My brother Walter married Minnie Paulson in 1939. They have three girls and three boys, Gladys Carol, Cherris, Tona Rae, Richard, Orville, and Charles. Walter and Minnie divorced when Charles, also known as Chuck, was about a year and a half. My brother was a womanizer and I am sure that is the reason for the divorce. He moved to Elko, Nevada and married a lady by the name of Pat. After two weeks of marriage she ran off with another man. Walter found his station wagon in San Jose, California. That marriage was annulled. He then moved back to South Dakota on the farm with Dad and Mom as Dad had a heart attack. Dad had gotten the home, farm, debts and all when Uncle Willie, his brother who was taking care of the farm, passed away. There were two houses on the farm so Walter had a house for his family again. Francis, Walter's second wife after divorcing Minnie, was very strict with the kids. Gladys and Cherris left home. But Francis was a good cook and very clean. But really liquor for both Walter and Francis caused their downfall. Dad ended up selling the home place and he and Mom moved to Rapid City, South Dakota. After two years there, Dad had a fatal heart attack.

Walter remarried to a lady named Vi. She died from diabetes and Walter remained in Oak Creek, Colorado until he was killed in a car accident in 1987. Dorthy, my sister, married James Wilcox and they have six children, four boys and two girls. They never lived around the rest of us much. James was a bodied and fender man. Of their children, Vernon lived in California. Robert died in Las Vegas in 1999. Billie lived in the desert in Las Vegas. There was no power or water but that's the way Billie liked to live. Billie sold aluminum cans and scrap metal to survive. Danny worked in a couple of trades. He was married and had two sons, Cody and Kyle. Linda married Ray Lingard. They have four girls and one boy.

One daughter died from epilepsy. Bonnie Mae married Frank Hastings and has a boy and a girl. Frank and Bonnie divorced and Frank was killed in an auto accident. Bonnie remarried. Her and her new husband were victims of a shooting. Both survived but are now separated. There were too many pressures. My baby sister, Mary Ruth, was named Mary Ruth because Mom's cousin Ruth and Dad's cousins wife, Mary, were the midwife nurses who delivered Mary Ruth without a doctor attending. Doctor Hurley was the old country doctor. Mary Ruth at age 16 married Jim Artz, who was 17. They celebrated their 50th wedding anniversary in October 1996. They are both gone now. They had five children. Kerry, Rick, Karla, Marilyn, and Penny. All live in the Minneapolis area, except Marilyn, who lives in Florida.

EULALIA BARTELS

Of course there is me, who married at the age of sixteen to David McCamly, who was age 25. We have Vonnie, whose birth name is Yvonne, Sharon, Ethel, Terry, and Dixie. One son, Francis Alvin, was born August 1941 and only lived eleven hours.

I will try to recall funny things that happened in my life as far back as I can remember. At the time of my birth, we were living four miles east of the Bartels' home place. There was a terrible blizzard when Mom went into labor. There weren't any telephones then, so Dad had to go with a team and sled to get Doc Hurley to come and get a midwife. I was born at one thirty in the morning on January 2, 1924. The reason for my name was because Mom had picked the other two names. Eulalia Breene was Dad's favorite school teacher. When he named me, Mom said, "How do you spell it?" My middle name being Ilene, made my brother tease me about my name. It would make me so mad. He was always teasing me because I was a "little spit fire" my folks said. Dorthy, my sister was always quiet and sat around a lot.

I remember Fred and Mary, my cousins, leaving their son Dean, with Mom and Dad. Dean and I would play house using an empty grain bin for our house. I have pictures of Dean and me with our wagon loaded with a little table, chairs made by Dad, doll buggy and dolls. We were moving to another house, really another grain bin.

Dorthy and I used to pretend we were riding horse back. We used a fifty gallon barrel tipped over for our horse. Our real horse back ride was only when we would go out to the field where Dad was working and on his way home, he would sit us on the work horses, Pride and Daisy.

When I was about three years old, my brother and sister were trying to teach me to say my name, "Eulalia". I would stomp my foot and say "Me Laala". When we had neighbors over, when I was about five, Mom and Dad would tell them about "Me Laala". I remember being so embarrassed, I would run and hide under the bed until someone came to get me.

We had a neighbor boy, Dale, who had to stay at our house after school until his dad was ready to go home because his dad was helping my dad build a grain storage. Dale was always throwing rocks and sticks at us girls. Finally, my dad said, "You don't have to put up with it. Just beat him up a little." So, Dorthy and I took him down and hit him. He wasn't mean anymore.

One time, in the middle of winter, when we had big snow banks, we would go out to play. Walter and Dorthy started snow balling me because I was the littlest. I picked up a small shovel, swore at them, and threw it at Walter. Once Mom was looking out the open window and heard me get upset and saw me throw the shovel at Walter. She came out of the house with a razor strap in her pocket. She spanked Walter first, then Dorthy and me last. I didn't get a very hard spanking, but cried just the same.

In the winter, when the snow was deep and the banks were up to the haystack and barn roof, we would go up the haystack onto the barn roof and slid down. It was so much fun and we would do this for hours, trying to see whose sled went the farthest before we would roll off the haystack or freeze with cold. In those days there wasn't any bales of hay.

Sometimes we would climb up the windmill tower and jump off into the snow. That was fun too, and sometimes we would sink in the snow so deep we had a hard time getting out. Sometimes we would dig all afternoon in the snow banks and make tunnels, either coming out the other side or making a little room. Then another blizzard comes up and there went our tunnel, either filled up with drifting snow or would move the whole snow bank if the wind was in a different direction.

Sometimes we would go down on to the frozen pond and with a little snow sprinkled around, the ice was very slippery. We would run and slide as far as we could. We didn't have ice skates. It was fun to play in the snow. So sledding down steep hills, have snowball fights, and make angels in the snow are what we did. Now, I hate the snow and cold weather.

We had to carry water up the hill from the well. Mom would send Dorthy and me with a twelve quart bucket each to get water. We had to pump it by hand of course. Well, I fell off the platform we stood on and hurt myself and being only about seven years old, I started crying and probably screaming. So Dorthy said, "Eulalia fell down and killed herself." That was between sobs. Mom said "You silly goose, if she killed herself she wouldn't be crying. Let's go to the house and put a cloth on her bruise."

My dad didn't want us girls to milk the cows. Mom did milk, but I guess that was different. One night, Dorthy and I decided we would get up real early and surprise Dad and have the cows milked. Not a very good idea. We didn't know we had to have a lot of strength in our hands and arms which we didn't at our young age. We picked a nice gentle cow and Dorthy would get a couple of squirts and then she'd get up and I would try. We really got a scolding when Dad came to the barn and saw what we were trying to do. Dad never spanked us, but for some reason when he said something and not gruffly, we knew he meant it and we would go back to our room.

One time when Mom and Dad went to get dressed for church we were all dressed in our church clothes. We went to the work shop and got into axle grease. We smeared it on the wall and wiped our hands on our clothes. Talk about being scolded, we sure did hear it that time. Walter got the worst tongue lashing as he knew better. Mom had a terrible time getting the stains out of our clothes. Mom and Aunt Elsa made our laundry soap out of hog fat, lye, and I don't know what else, but they always made it outside over a low fire and I remember them taking turns stirring and then when done, it was spread out. As soon as it hardened they cut it into bars and divided up the soap. We had to stay far back so no lye would splatter on us.

When I was nine, Uncle Willie passed away. We moved on to Grandpa Bartels' farm and Dad had to take over all the debts Uncle Willie left, but Dad also got Uncle Willie's cattle and machinery, so that helped. After the funeral, Aunt Elsie left and moved to Huron, South Dakota and never returned to Gettysburg to my knowledge. She left her piano at least.

I can remember the house parties that were held in the winter months. My Uncle Ralph, Uncle Jack, Mom and sometimes Dad suited off to play music for dancing. Our house had a large dining room and living room with highly polished wood floors. Mom's cousins also had rooms large enough for neighborhood dancing. Dad taught us to Waltz, Two-step, and Schottische when I was six years old. Mom and Dad won a waltz contest in the auditorium in Gettysburg when I was about twelve. My cousin Doris would have won but because of our ages and both being girls, we didn't. We girls had neighbor boyfriends to dance with.

The country school we went to was just across the road but even then in storming, blizzard days school would be closed as the other kids had a ways to go. The most number of kids in the school in a year was twelve. All eight grades in the same classroom. I believe we learned a lot by listening to the other grade classes. School was from nine in the morning to four in the evening with two recesses and an hour for lunch. We went home for lunch but hurried back so we could go back and play games. I wasn't allowed to school at the age of five because my birthday was past the beginning of the year. Later it was changed. You had to be six by November first.

Two different years the school teacher boarded at our house. Talk about being crowded in a two bedroom house. We had two beds in Mom and Dad's room for Dorthy and I to share. Mary Ruth's crib was in the kitchen. Walter had a cot in the living room so the teacher had the other bedroom. She spent most of the evening in her room correcting papers and preparing tests. Everyone had to go outside to the outdoor toilet. No such thing as running water in those days. We didn't take a bath everyday. Usually Sunday was bath time to be clean and our hair sometimes curled by a curling iron heated over the kerosene lamp.

Dorthy had to start wearing glasses at the age of eleven. I was twelve when I had to start wearing them. My brother started wearing glasses at a young age too. Dad never wore glasses except to read when he got to be about sixty. Mom wore glasses after they were married. None of us went to contacts after they were available. We were too old for a change and couldn't afford them then.

A family friend of my folks Bill Schmaltz, worked for Dad and he had this beautiful white horse. "Gently" was his name. One day Bill set me in the saddle and the horse took off for the barn. The big door was open and Bill about had a heart attack as he thought the horse would run right into the barn. I can remember seeing the top of the door casing and thinking it would hit my head and knock me off. But when Gently got to the door, he stopped and waited for Bill to get there. He never put me on his horse again. It was scary.

Mom had Uncle Willie's collie dog. We'd say "Go get the cow!" He wouldn't run them but just trail along behind and keep them all together in a line. Mom had to drive us to school four miles after we moved. In nice weather, we walked home. Dorthy graduated from the 8th grade. Mom bought her a dark blue silk dress for graduation night in case it rained. Mom had Aunt Nellie make her a pretty summery flowered dress if it was a nice night.

I carried a three gallon can of water to school in my 8th year. School house was close as they used my Grandma's house for a school for a couple of years. I got 17.80 at the end of the year from the county school system. I had to buy my own dress, shoes, slip, nylons. I even had enough left for a wrist watch. I was able to buy all for 17.00. My dress was royal blue silk with pitched pleats in front. Walter and Dorthy always got new things and I took the hand me down of Dorthy's. Dorthy talked her out of her new watch since her watch was big and she had to use a pair of pliers to wind it.

After Dorthy started high school, she stayed at Grandma Johnson's in town the first two years. I rode horse back on my cousin's horse "Patty" for miles to school, until the snow got too deep and then I stayed at Uncle Han's who had moved onto our old place just across the road from the school. In the Spring, I would meet the neighbor kids from the north who rode horses. They always wanted to race and I couldn't hold Patty back. She wouldn't let their horses beat her. I was always afraid she would stumble as we road down the hill. Patty was 20 years old. One night my cousin Elsie wanted to ride Patty, so she got out another horse to ride back when we got to the end of their pasture. So I rode the other horse that far. When she got off Patty, Patty took off for our place. I had to walk two miles home. When Dad saw the horse come home without me they were worried something had happened to me. Mom came and found me walking. Boy, did I catch it. Patty was so gentle that when Elsie, Violet, and I all rode her and we all fell off under her, Patty would stop and let us get up. Then we had a hard time getting back on with nothing to stand on, as we were riding bare back and couldn't jump that far. But, finally we got her close enough to the fence and each one of us made it back on. Such fun we had.

When I was in the 7th grade, Mary Ruth was in the first. We had to stay at Uncle Bill and Aunt Elsie's and walked two and a half miles to school, as our school had been closed due to not enough kids in the South Lowell district to keep it open so we went to North Lowell. One day a blizzard came, so Uncle Bill and cousin Edward came after us with a team and sleigh. I stood up and drove the team half way home as Uncle Bill's and Edward's faces and hands were freezing. My cousin Doris, daughter to Bill and Elsie, Mary Ruth, and cousin Bob were sitting in straw and covered up with a quilt. Doris frosted her legs and got white blisters. Uncle Bill and Edward each had frost bite on their faces but I never froze any part of my face or hands. Neither did Mary Ruth nor Bob. It was strange that the men got frost bite since they were used to the cold feeding cattle and hogs.

My 7th and 8th grade years were spent in my grandmother's house converted to a classroom. The teachers had a bedroom and the other bedroom was our library. The kitchen was our cloak room. Everything at the time was running normally like families do. Hard work on the farm. It was our job to chop wood and gather corn cobs to burn in the range and heater. Dorthy hated to be outside so she would bribe me into doing that while she gathered the eggs. She would also wash the supper dishes. That was in the summer and on weekends when she was home from school in town.

When Dorthy was about twelve, Dad decided she should learn how to drive our Model A Ford. She could steer it all right but had a terrible time trying to shift gears. I rode in the back seat and Dad had her drive down a county road and when she had to shift to a lower gear, she would have a hard time. I reached up over the seat and put it in the gear she needed. Dad yelled at me to sit down. When he yelled, we knew we had better listen although he never hit us or spanked us.

My brother Walter always picked on me because I was a little spit fire. One time my cousin Roy and Walter took Dorthy and me to a movie. It was "Frankenstein". I got so scared, I crawled upon Roy's lap and hid my eyes. He teased me about it for years. First, Uncle Hans moved from Potter County to Waverly, South Dakota.

Then Aunt Nellie and Uncle Albert moved to Kranburg, South Dakota, which was about ten miles from Uncle Hans. I got to take my one and only train ride from Gettysburg to Watertown where Uncle Hans picked me up. I had just finished the 5th grade. I was so scarred, alone on the train. I was afraid I might get off at the wrong station and be lost. But another lady was going most of the way and she looked after me. Later, the lady, Nina Eldean, married your grandpa's second cousin, Sid Wager. They got married the same week David and I did. So did Lucille Herrin and Orville Ellenbucher, so we had a wedding dance at the Community Club for all three couples on Saturday night. My David only danced square dances, so my dad danced the first dance with me. Ah, well here I am ahead of my story again.

I spent eight weeks with Aunt Nellie and Uncle Albert that summer. I wanted to help Aunt Nellie stock the grain for threshing so she let me go to the field with her. I only lasted a couple of hours and I went back to the house and stayed in the shade. Aunt Nellie had told me to dust the furniture and floors. The floor was varnished and shiny. Well, I dusted, but not under the furniture. When she came in and saw the dust under the stand she scolded me and like a kid, I said "I'm doing this!" She was flabbergasted to hear me swear at her. I sometimes fixed sandwiches for their lunch and fried chicken and vegetables from the garden for dinner. To us, it was "supper" and not dinner. One day we had a terrible lightning and wind storm. I saw the lightning hit the barn, but no damage to it as there was a hay cable from the hay door to the ground and the lightning followed down the cable and didn't set the barn on fire. Uncle Albert drank quite a bit on Saturday night, but never had an accident. He sold tickets at the dance hall in Kanzburg, so I got to go to the dance quite often. The neighbor to the north had a couple of sons and of course I thought Felix was sweet on me as he danced with me a lot.

One of my dreams was to be a school teacher, so when we went to Watertown shopping, we'd go to the Five and Dime store and Aunt Nellie bought me spelling books, arithmetic books and sometimes just fairy tales. I spent hours in my room pretending I was a teacher.

When I was in the 8th grade, after graduation and one week of working for the neighbors, I went back to Aunt Nellie's for six weeks. She bought and made me some clothes to start high school. I was able to do a better job of housekeeping for her by then. She always wore shirt and overalls, as she helped Uncle Albert all the time with farm work. That was the last time I spent time with them as I was then ready for high school.

While in the 4-H Club, I took our car without Mother knowing and went for a ride. I was never taught how to drive but I instinctively knew how. I was always observant of what was going on around me. I still am. Dorthy was a senior when I was a freshman. We stayed with Grandma Johnson. We were always glad in the winter time when we heard the fire alarm go off, meaning no school because there was a blizzard. When I was in the 8th grade, I won the county spelling contest and advanced to the state. But the county superintendent that took two of us girls to the state couldn't spell a lot of the words given that day. So both Faye Ellen Sloat and I didn't win the state.

My first year of high school I was in the 4-H Club and won county for sewing. I missed the first few days of high school when I was a sophomore to go to the State Fair. Well, I didn't win there either, but it was an honor to win at the county level.

I wasn't an honor student by far. I quit high school in April, after eighteen months of dating David McCamly. We broke up once but went back together. I never was popular in school as we were the poor family from the country. There were poor families in town too. But living in the country and not being around many people, my sister and I were very bashful and didn't fit into the elite clubs or groups. We never had a date with another high school boy. School was not exciting to me at all there, however, as I stated before, I did want to be a teacher.

I quit school March 30, 1940 and David and I were married April 19, 1940. He was nine years and ten and a half months older. Times were bad so we lived with Granddad McCamly on a farm seventeen miles southeast of town. Our minister lived in Lebanon, South Dakota, but was the pastor of the Gettysburg Lutheran Church also. I wrote Reverend Frueger and asked him to marry us at my folks home on April 19th at 5:00 pm. The mailman dropped the letter and just that day a young boy found it laying in the gutter. So, we almost didn't get married. Also, David had a hair-raising experience on his way out to my folks. He was driving down a steep hill and the bridge was full of a herd of horses. He was driving about ninety miles an hour on the gravel road and no way could he stop. The car had twin horns, so he laid on the horns and the horses split and he went between them. I ran from the car to the house, but on the way I stopped and went to the outdoor toilet. We didn't have an indoor one. I stopped and fell and just rolled in the dirt and grass. So our day ended fine after all the problems. Sounds odd but that night we went to the neighbors and the men played cards late. We got down to David's father's house and got to bed about three am. We stayed in bed until two thirty the next afternoon. When David went to the garage, there were two flat tires on the car. I don't know if all these things happening at the special moments of one's life was unforeseen better times or was meant to be an omen of worse times to come.

My brother Walter and Minnie were married in my folks living room on June 1939, our marriage April 1940 and sister Dorthy and Jim on March 1941. But when baby sister Mary Ruth and Jim got married, they married in a Catholic church in Gettysburg as Jim was Catholic. So Mom and Dad's family reduced quite a bit in twenty one months. The dry years were over and three of us being gone made life a little easier for mom and dad.

David and I lived with Granddad McCamly for the first four years of marriage. We had Vonnie. We then had Sharon, Ethel, and at last a son, Terry, then came Dixie. After our first year, we acquired an FHA loan and bought sheep and hogs to get us started. Grandad McCamly had milk cows, so that paid for the groceries along with the eggs sold. We immediately planted a garden and being World War II was in full battle, I made part of the garden into a flower bed and planted them in the shape of a "V" for victory. Beings David was twenty six, he wasn't called into the military because of his age and being a farmer. David would go to town and get drunk and not come home by chore time, so he would come in from the field and have to milk cows. I couldn't see him doing it alone, so I learned how to milk cows too. The cows were all gentle and Vonnie would sit on the ground on a blanket in the barnyard while we milked cows. After Sharon was born, I didn't have to milk very often while we lived there. When we got our own milk cows I always helped with the milking. David and Granddad McCamly both drank quite heavily. Many times I milked the cows, about twelve of them, by myself in the evening because they were in town drinking. Finally, when one time they were put in jail and I refused to milk alone again in the morning. I took the kids to town and I went to the jail and said "Give me some money so we can go eat breakfast." David was angry because I hadn't milked the cows. They got out of jail in the afternoon and his sister Olive, who is quite high class, was at the house. They were very embarrassed. That is the only time they were ever put in jail. This drinking, which we certainly couldn't afford, went on for eight years of marriage.

When I was pregnant with Terry, they were in town drinking again. David thought I called him to come home now as I was in labor. Well, I never called which he claimed I did, and raced home. He had a car accident. Not serious but enough so a neighbor brought him home and we went back and got the car, which was driveable. He had to go back to town and get Granddad McCamly as David left him there. I again made him help milk the cows before we went back to town. Many times in the winter, I would not go to town for weeks at a time. The men went every Saturday, came home to milk the cows, bring the groceries, eat supper and go back to town. They would come home at midnight when the pool hall closed.

On David's birthday, when it was approaching our ninth year of marriage, a man came and picked him up and took him along to North Dakota to buy turkeys. They were drinking all day and we were to go to a birthday party for David at some people's house, who had a birthday in their family also. I did not go out and milk the cows, so when the men finally came home, Uncle Herman said it was his fault. He stayed and helped milk the cows. Granddad McCamly stayed home with the kids and we left for the party about nine in the evening. We just started down the road and David pulled a bottle of whiskey out from under the seat and some 7-Up and said, "Mix us up a drink." I replied "No, I don't want any." David tapped me on the leg and said "I don't either." He threw the whiskey out the window and never drank liquor or beer again. Granddad McCamly quit then too but started again in a year or so. He didn't get drunk too often but drank beer when he went to town and until he reached seventy-five when he stopped again and never took it up.

David was so slow getting around in the morning. I would be outside getting the milk cows in and starting to milk before he would get out of bed. One time it was about thirty degrees below zero when I went to the milk barn. I sat down to the first cow and when I got up from her I bumped her stomach with the pail and she started kicking and tearing around. I spilled milk all over me. Needless to say my clothes froze stiff as a board. I sat right down on the other side of that cow and milked my sixth cow when David came to the barn. I was so upset and cold.

When Dixie was about four months old, Granddad McCamly had to have an emergency appendicitis operation so he wasn't able to work in the field. That's when I started driving the tractors. I ran every piece of machinery except the combine harvester and the hay baler. We had a bale sled that we pulled behind the bales. I rode that and stacked the bales in stacks of twelve, took a crow bar and jammed it between the planks and slid the bales off as we kept going and had to be ready to catch the next bale and start another stack of twelve. This was not very easy work. All David had to do was sit on the tractor and follow the rows of hay and watch for rocks so the baler wouldn't pick them up and break something. This was in the heat of summer. I would go six miles from home, alone, and mow hay all day. I would come home and to the routine of chores, dinner and more. I had to mow hay where the land was rocky. I hit a rock twice with the front wheel of the tractor and broke it off. I used to have to go after repairs right from the field and I was dirty. My clothes would be filthy. I was embarrassed but that was part of being a farmer. One time my tractor wouldn't start so I had to crank it. When it started, it kicked the crank backwards and bent both my thumbs back. I thought for sure they were broken and here I was alone and six miles from home. I rubbed them a while and got back on the tractor and worked until five o'clock in the evening. My thumbs weren't even sprained. It didn't matter, I had to milk the cows anyway.

Needless to say, David got better about getting up in the morning. He got neuritis in his one arm and said he couldn't stand it to milk the cows. So I proceeded to keep on. Vonnie was old enough so she had been helping with the chores and house work.

On Saturday, while we were in the field, the girls had to clean house. Vonnie was going to bring our lunch to us. We were harvesting our crop six miles away from home. Vonnie butchered a spring fryer and decided to bake bread. This was her first attempt. Well, she didn't read all the directions, which I guess she gets from me. It said to scald the milk and let it cool to lukewarm. She didn't let it cool and added the yeast to it. Low and behold, it killed the yeast, so her first loaf of bread didn't rise. She baked it and brought our lunch. The bread tasted good, but heavy. She felt bad.

While David was still drinking and Dorthy and Jim lived in Gettysburg, we always went to Mobridge, South Dakota on the fourth of July. We had our niece, Darleen Tobin, stay with the kids. We didn't have too many kids then and took another niece, Mary Tobin, along. We went to the usual parade and celebration. We would sometimes go to the rodeo, if they weren't too drunk by then. Granddad McCamly and Grandpa David mixed drinks on the way, they gave Mary drinks too and she was a teenager. When we got there, which was forty miles away, Mary was getting pretty unstable. We met our friends, Ben and Gen Shoups, there. Well, you might know where the men and Dorthy were. Dorthy drank heavily then. In the bar, I had to walk Mary around and sober her up and then we stayed in Ben and Gen's care. Gen and I watched their kids. Of course when Ben took off for the bathroom for a while and Grandpa David didn't know where I was, he accused me and Ben of slipping off somewhere. We finally got started for home late in the evening about ten o'clock.

It had stormed and rained hard. On the way, David and Granddad got into an argument. I was driving and had to stop. They got out to fight and then they realized they were father and son. Then Dorthy and Jim got into an argument and Dorthy got into a crying spell. Fun, fun!! When I went to turn into our driveway, there were two ways to go once you turned. I was going on the little grade, when David said "No, go in on the other road," which had a big water hole. Of course, we got stuck in the mud and that was my fault, he said. We had to get our feet wet to get to the house. David was drunk. He passed out on the hide-a-bed that we needed to open up to put the kids on. He got mad when I was getting him up and he fell on the floor. He backed me up against the wall with his hand on my throat. Dorthy made him stop. Jim and I went out to milk the cows at midnight and Granddad came down and accused Jim and I of making out. He was at one cow in the yard and me at another. The more I did when David was drinking, the more he accused me of wrong doing.

After he quit drinking life became dull because our friends quit coming to visit as the men all drank. We did hold some card parties in the winter and go to some. The Shoups did remain our best friends.

One year I raised six hundred frying chickens. I advertised them and had to dress them out, about fifty every Saturday morning. We sold most and froze some for ourselves. I would get up at two o'clock Saturday morning to have the chickens ready for packaging in time to milk the cows.

We had this one dog, English Boxer, that was like a mother to any baby, human, calf, lamb or chicken. She tried to mother them all. She killed thirty-one of my baby chicks trying to mother them. She finally had puppies. The first batch we gave most of them away. We sold one and the Walkins man ran over one and his insurance paid for it. Later, she got an infection and first all puppies died and then she died.

In December 1944, we moved into my parents place as they had gone to Kansas and worked in a gun powder plant. Well, Granddad couldn't stand living alone, so he sold his farm and bought one six miles from my folks and we moved in there when Mom and Dad got back from Kansas. We farmed together and got an FHA loan and bought more livestock and machinery. In 1958 we bought the farm from Granddad and he went to work for another farmer to get some paid into Social Security. As soon as Granddad could, he bought a small house in Gettysburg and still worked quite a few years for the other farmers. His social security was minimal, like 129.00 a month. But his house was paid for and so were his two cars. The power or groceries weren't so expensive then so he mad out okay. He rented his house out when he went into the nursing home. He was satisfied there as he and his roommate played cards a lot, until the other man was moved to another room and later passed away. Granddad passed in 1977. His house was then given to his daughter Eldora and her husband, Joe. They lived there quite a few years before Joe passed away. She remained there for a while but then moved into a low income apartment complex and at the age of 89 moved into a nursing home.

Anyway, after we purchased the farm, hard times really hit. We had not enough rains to have enough grass for the cattle and had to buy feed and only pastured the cattle three months of the year. We had just gotten our machinery all paid for and we asked for a loan to operate the farm another year, but was turned down and was told we had to pay back 5,000 dollars from the year before. David came in the house and told me that and said "What will we do? Sell out?" I said "Yes" immediately. I had always dreamed of living in town. I had worked hard to make a living but many times dreamed of being a teacher and living in town. Well, living in town came to be. My dream of being a teacher came to be when in 1962 we moved to Las Vegas, Nevada and I trained all those girls to be telephone operators.

I think I may have missed some of our ups and downs in our romance before David and I were married. I met David through a friend. The first night he and his cousin took a car load of us young people to Agar, South Dakota to dance. Beings he didn't dance, he stayed out in the car. His girlfriend went in and danced so I went back out and sat in the car for a while and we got acquainted. David was working in Gettysburg and we were staying in town and going to high school, so I saw him after school and we talked some more. Well, he dropped his girlfriend and we started going together. Back in those days, just going riding up and down the street was a date. After going with David for about a year, he met some of our high school friends and he fell for this one girl, June, but instead her sister, Dorthy May intruded and always sat in the middle. She was talking about marriage and he wanted no part of that. He would put his arm around June and hold Dorthy May's hand. He told me that several times. Well, Dorthy May was younger than me, so she really was too young for him. June and David broke up and he came back to me. We went out for a year and a half before we got married. One time before we were married, David wasn't around after the dance ended, I had some other guys from Lowery to take me home. As we drove in the yard, David drove in and a fist fight occurred. Well, he got a black eye from one of the guys before throwing the guy off the place. It wasn't their fault as they just brought me home on time. My folks really liked David a lot, even though they didn't ever drink and David did. Well, I kind of filled in a few missing tales that I forgot as I went along.

I always had dreams and hopes of being a school teacher and residing in town. The size of town never occurred to me at an early age of any town being bigger than Gettysburg, which grew from a beginning back in the 1800's. Sometime it grew to the size of seventeen hundred people. Now, at this time, it is down to about fifteen hundred people. Many people I knew are gone now and not many relatives back there anymore. I have four cousins there. One is at Sturgis, South Dakota, one at Rapid City, South Dakota and one at Roscoe, South Dakota and one in New York someplace. I have a sister-in-law and one niece. One nephew in Oneida, South Dakota. There is a nephew in Black Horse, South Dakota and also somewhere in Wyoming. So there isn't too much reason to go back there. The Tabin reunions are almost to a halt now with Eldora in the nursing home and Darleen, Pat, and Donnie already deceased.

Must get back on track with goings on in my life. We purchased the farm from Granddad McCamly, in 1957. We already had our machinery for farming and a herd of cattle, along with some hogs and chickens. We didn't have much rain to make the crops and grass grow and we had no irrigation in our area. We planned on selling our farm.

So we went to town and talked to the auctioneer, Herman Peayell, and he advised us on how to proceed with listing the sale. We went back home and listed as much as we could think of and the next day took the list to the printers. A week later we went to several towns within a one hundred mile and passed the sale bills. Our sale was on Tuesday, March 21, 1962. Well, naturally nothing can run smoothly. On Sunday the 19th, we had a blizzard. On Monday, Ben Shoup scooped snow all day to clear paths to the farm for sale. We cleared twenty thousand dollars. At this time, we had been married 22 years. We traded our car and pickup for a new 1962 Chevy and then made arrangements to have the kids stay with Vonnie, our eldest daughter, and husband Al. We took our first honeymoon and traveled for six weeks ending up in Las Vegas, Nevada.

I needed to get a job so I looked in the paper and found an add for "Earn as you learn, Southern Nevada Telephone Company". I went for an interview and the lady said that I would have to take a test, which was on math, English, and geography. So I passed the test with a ninety five percent and she said, "Huh, I guess farm girls aren't so dumb." I never forgot this incident. David went to work at a laundry as a sorter and worked thirty nine months until he got the job with the city. He worked for thirteen years before he retired. He retired eleven years before he got sick.

The years went by and we did some gambling. We met Dick and Dee Bright. We had known Dee back in South Dakota. We were friends with her parents. Her aunt Gen and Uncle Ben Shoup were our best friends. We quite often played cards with them and had some delicious meals there.

The years go by. In July 1988, David passed away. I made up my mind I wasn't going to sit at home and be a television buff. Some women start drinking from loneliness. Not me. I missed out on a lot of dating and dancing by getting married so young. I wanted to meet someone who was a good dancer. I had met Al Ryan bowling and he was a very nice escort for dinner but he was also a gigolo. I had to pay the way all the time. I went back to South Dakota and spent three months there. I stayed at Howard Maroney's, a dear friend. He took me to the Moose Club dancing. He was a good dancer. We had some good times. He came to Las Vegas in the winter for one year. We went to California to his sister, Deloris, and back down from his aunt's funeral. We also had some nice times but he wouldn't make a commitment to me and I know why. He knew he had cancer but wouldn't tell me. He didn't want me to go through what I had gone through with David. He passed away two years after we had been together. He was in the veteran's hospital in Sioux Falls, South Dakota and I didn't go back there. Al Ryan passed away April 2000. I couldn't stand Al and he irritated me to no end. In August 1989 my friend, Helen asked me if I wanted to work part time. She worked at a doughnut shop. I put in my application and was hired the next morning. The first day I worked, I met Tom. He was an employee there for about three years. We didn't start seeing each other except at work until November. He was also working the office of the motel where he lived. The motel was also known as "Cock Roach Haven" and he wanted to get out of there. He asked if he could rent my spare bedroom. That's when we started living together. We were just companions. Sometimes we would disagree but mostly our thinking was about the same.

I got upset at the owner of the doughnut shop because he wouldn't fix the hot water heater and I was expected to clean greasy doughnut-making equipment. I was also to wait on customers and make muffins all in four hours time. For two days I put down thirty minutes overtime and he crossed it out and wrote "Not Authorized". When he came in I took off my apron and cap and said "I don't need this." He said "What?" I quit and walked out the door. I was there fifteen months. In February he pulled bad things on Tom so he quit too. By June, Tom hadn't looked for a job and he was not old enough for Social Security so I started looking for something we could do together. So the first thing we did was deliver telephone books. Then we started delivering Avon. After fifteen months, Tom was offered to haul heavy freight if he got a big truck. We also had two step vans I had bought. We then hired a young man and he messed up someway and got money off our gasoline credit card so he left town in a hurry. But beings it was under fifty dollars we didn't report it to the police. Then Tom's ex-son-in-law brought Pat Gallahan over and he drove the step van for a year or so. We traded the van for a '93 box truck. Well, Pat decided he wanted to be a bar tender again, so another guy drove for a while. He used the truck for personal use and had a slight accident. That cost me three hundred dollars to settle. Then Pat came back and wanted to drive again and stay with me and Tom. He has been with me ever since. In February, I believe, the big freight truck ended and we finally traded the truck in for another GMC van. Tom had been a trucker for thirty-two years so he finally started using the pickup and delivering Avon again. I had been doing Avon deliveries all this time. I hired a lady to help me and then got the new van. We had three vehicles delivering Avon. Tom finally got a chance to work for the Review Journal. He delivered for them, but not newspapers. He also drove to businesses and picked up checks from businesses.

I continued to deliver Avon, but due to a small accident, my legs and arms bothered me too much to lift those heavy boxes and Corporate Express gave me a job delivering light weight toners and supplies for copy machines. Sometimes we were involved with other type of deliveries. It is interesting to see so many different types of businesses. Many times I would ask what type of business it was. They kept me busy five days a week and I drove about a hundred miles a day in town. The traffic was bad but the pay was good. I get paid every other week. Last week, which had eleven days on the pay period, I made 1,115. Of course I have to pay for my own gas, insurance, and up keep and will pay my own income tax, medical, and Social Security taxes.

While doing other jobs, I also worked part time at San Francisco's Bridal Shop. Some interesting, funny, or embarrassing happenings occurred. Two English men came in to get a tuxedo for the one. He went in the dressing room and tried on the pants. He came out and said that they didn't feel right. So, I got him another pair to try on. Instead of going into the dressing room, he just stripped off the ones he had on. He stood right there and changed. They weren't satisfactory either, so I gave him another pair, same thing, except these fit fine. He wasn't embarrassed at all changing right there in the main part of the store. Then this French girl came in and tried on wedding gowns. Now I put the full slip on her after she had on the gown. Well, I pulled up the slip and she did not have any underpants on. I was shocked, but that happened several times after that.

One day, this tall man came in to try on wedding gowns. He had a long straight wig, a dress, sandals, lipstick, the whole list. Well, we always ask the bride if she needs assistance, so I said "Do you need help?" He did not. He never came back and did not rent that gown.

One other day, a heavy set man came in and he needed to rent a gown. Said he was going to dress like the bride and the bride dress like the groom. He needed our largest gown, size twenty-nine. Anyway, his wedding was the future and a couple of days later Lou Ann, owner of the shop, saw him and another man in a rather cozy situation.

Another guy came and tried on bride maids dresses. Just recently, two guys came in. They were military and were on a scavenger hunt and part of it was to dress in a bridal gown and have a picture taken. Well, he gave me a 20 tip for that. I met a lot of very nice people on my courier service route but fate was against me. I had this motor vehicle accident which told me to retire. This was 2001.

MY CHILDREN

Before I go farther with my life, I will fill in the happenings to each member of the family. My children are the most important part of my world. I mothered six children, Vonnie, Sharon, Ethel, Terry, Dixie, and Francis Alvin. Vonnie being the oldest, I will start with her. She really didn't have too many things happen that I can think of, other than her car accident. She was old enough to drive to town to school. We didn't have money enough to pay her school insurance which wasn't very much, but since she was working at Toby's Cafe, she could pay it. We would pay her back as soon as we sold some wheat. So she paid it on Monday. On Wednesday morning, on the way to school, she rolled the car and was nearly killed. The doctor would not give us any hope for four days. She was in the hospital for three weeks. She had to have her lungs tapped at least once after she got out of the hospital. I stayed at the hospital the first night. Her teacher stayed the second night. We had a special nurse the next two nights until she was out of danger. Her dad left with a neighbor boy that was on his way to school, who came back and told David of the wreck. David didn't say a word, just left. I happened to come out of the house before the neighbor boy left and he told me. I got transportation for the kids to go to school and Granddad McCamly took me to town. David didn't even remember going down town for lunch that day. I never couldn't really forgive him for not thinking about me, that I would naturally want to be at the hospital too. I was deeply hurt by his actions. When Vonnie got home and ready to go back to school, she drove the car we had bought from Granddad. She drove faster than when the wreck occurred. When the wreck happened she was only going about forty miles an hour. Her pencil fell onto the floor and she was trying to retrieve it when she misguided and went out of control. Other than childhood diseases, she didn't have too much bad luck.

Sharon seemed to have more problems. Vonnie and Sharon were running through the house and Sharon tripped and fell with her hand on the hot-pot bellied stove. David took her to the doctor in town. Then, one day after we moved to the farm the kids were raised on, we had gone to town because it was misty and rainy and couldn't do field work. When we got home we told the kids to stay in the house because we had chores to do. Well, they didn't mind and came out and climbed up on the grain drill. Sharon's muddy shoes hung and her foot slipped and she gashed her leg on a wheel scraper. No hospital in town at that time, so I called my mom, who was a practical nurse. She came down and cleaned the cut, pulled it together with tape and bandaged it. Before her leg was healed, she climbed up on the cupboard. I hollered at her to get down before she got hurt again and her reply was "That's okay. Grandma will fix it." One day, Vonnie wanted to iron hankies and Sharon got on a chair to watch. Well, Vonnie dropped the hot iron on Sharon's leg. She seemed to be doomed to get burned. One day, Vonnie and Sharon were running around the oil heater when Vonnie turned Sharon around to go the opposite way and that made Sharon lose her balance and she fell with her cheek against the hot stone pipe. One day when Vonnie, Sharon, and Ethel were all sick with bad colds and cramps, I put them on the bed and made a tent with a sheet. I put our Benzinito burner into the tent to create some steam. Well, Vonnie thought Sharon wasn't getting enough steam, so she picked up the steamer and the benzone spilled on Sharon's face. Poor Vonnie, she always seemed to be the one to cause Sharon to get burned. Sharon had an appendicitis operation and a tonsillectomy. Ethel and Vonnie had a tonsillectomy on the same day as Sharon. All were in the same room. Sharon was never as agile and didn't play outside as much. Sharon was in high school when on a Saturday, she cleaned house for me and rearranged the furniture in the living room. Ethel and Dixie were being tricky and put the furniture a different way. This made Sharon mad. She went upstairs and packed her suitcase and walked down the highway. We came home from the field and Sharon was gone. Of course, Ethel and Dixie thought that was funny. David went and picked her up and took her to town to her granddad's. I made Dixie and Ethel stand and listen to me about some stranger who might pick her up and then we would never see her again. Well, it made the girls cry. They seemed to enjoy picking on her. One day, they chased her. She climbed up on the roof of the barn. Kids! Oh my! Sometimes I wonder why I had them, but then we loved them just the same. Sharon, Ethel, and Ethel's boyfriend Wayne had a wreck one day, but no one was hurt. Now it's Ethel's turn. She had a few months of collapsing in a fainting spell. She was about three years old. We took her to Doctor Collins and he gave her a prescription of some bad-tasting little pills and it straightened her out fine. She had most childhood diseases. She was always small for her age. She was a little "spit fire" and a trouble maker. If she could get one of the other kids in trouble, she would. She was never guilty of mischief. From the time she was about twelve, she had a derogatory attitude. When she was fifteen, she said "No one would ever have me." Well, we came to Las Vegas and she met Tom Miller the first day we arrived. It was love at first sight. Much to our chagrin, it lasted twenty-seven years and ended with much bitterness. Tom really changed. I guess you call it the "change of life", which use to be called "menopause" in women, but men can have this too. She remarried but that was a big mistake.

Terry, our only son except for Francis Alvin, our last. The girls say he was a spoiled. I have always tried to treat each one alike. There is always something seen by others that we aren't aware of. Of course, his dad was so glad to have a son. I knew he favored him in his younger years. When he was about six years old, Ethel, Dixie, and Terry were playing and the girls had their dolls and buggy. An old sow started after them so they climbed a tree, dolls, buggy and all. Terry fell out and broke his collar bone. One time, he had a pull fracture of one elbow when he was climbing into a manger in the barn when he was three years old. He was nicknamed "Tubby" or "Teddy Tumbleweed". When Terry was four or five years old, we had a rooster that would chase the kids some. He was coming across the hog lot, coming up to where we were stacking hay bales, when the rooster came after him.

He said, "I'm not afraid of that old rooster." But Terry was stomping his feet and screaming. Everyone teased him about not being afraid of that old rooster. One time he hit Vonnie on the head with a baseball bat. I went to spank him, he started running and ran up to the neighbors where his dad was. When they got home, I had forgotten about it. Ethel never forgot how Terry didn't get spanked. We started Terry in school at five years of age as he would be six on November first. Well, the county said you had to be six by November first so the teacher made him quit. The next year we had a very poor teacher. All she could think about was her boyfriend. She never taught him to read well, which made some classes hard for him. He got old enough to help a lot on the farm. Terry would milk the cows, drive the tractor and jeep. We would find skid marks in the pasture where he was going too fast and turned but luckily he never wrecked the jeep. When we moved to Las Vegas, he worked for Mission Linen before he was old enough. They asked for his birth certificate and we said we had to send to South Dakota for it. They never asked again. He worked about two months and then started high school. He avoided school too many times and eventually was expelled. He has always been a hard worker. Terry and his friends, Craig, Kenny and Don were taken to juvenile hall one night. The cops thought they had tried to break into the East Las Vegas Post Office. Well, I got Terry, Craig, and Kenny out in time early the next morning, as Terry had to go to work. They kept Don in jail til later that day and David went and got him. Don also went to court and was put in our custody temporarily. Don lived with us afterwards. Terry met Carla, his wife, at a store, Kresges, when he worked there. One day, Carla shot herself in the shoulder and called for Terry to come. He went, of course, and could have been blamed for shooting her. She survived but it didn't miss her heart by very far. Terry had a habit of dropping Dixie off at school and didn't go in when she did. Said he was going to have a smoke first. Then he would leave and miss school. He lost his driver's license, but was upset his car didn't start right. He would drive to his friends' house, Steven and Butch. Butch would drive but that day he drove and ran a stop sign with seven high school kids in the car. He managed to swing the car around enough so the loaded gravel truck ran over the back corner of the car. Dixie was hurt the most, but only temporarily lost consciousness. She told the policeman "Don't arrest my brother." Well, he lost his license for a year. I was working for the telephone company at the time. When the telephone call came in at the telephone company, the supervisor came and told me about the wreck. They said I turned white as a ghost. David was down stairs waiting for me. One time, while Terry didn't have his license back, I let him take our car to his dad, who was in South Dakota. I never slept a wink until he got back home. Guess I kind of told tales on Terry, huh.

Now we get around to Dixie. She was born one day and seven years later than Sharon. Sharon was born on Granddad McCamly's birthday and Dixie one day apart. Vonnie and Ethel were born one day before their dad, David's, birthday and five years apart. Got off the track again. When Dixie was six months old, she got infected and was hospitalized for a week. She had already been in the hospital a week with pneumonia when she was three weeks old. All went well until she was a year and a half old. Her dad was going out and plowing in the field until midnight so I made some coffee for him to take and decided to have a cup myself. Well, Dixie's fingers reached up and grabbed the cup and the hot coffee spilled on her. I finally got her undressed and the skin peeled off her chest. David had not left yet for the field, so we took her to Hoven to the hospital. She was in there for two weeks. While in there, the neighbor boy was put in the children's ward with the measles. Well, Dixie got the measles. Besides the burn healing and itching, she had the measles too. The hospital tried to deny she got the measles there but when I told them it was Wayne Halzworth, the neighborhood boy, they had to admit it. We went on a trip to Lawrence, Kansas where my folks were working while Dixie was in the hospital. Our niece came out and stayed with the other kids and milked the cows and fed the chickens. Our niece has left this world now at the age of sixty-two. Cigarettes gave her emphysema. She also had some heart problems. When Dixie was six years old, she had to have her appendix removed. When she was nine years old, she had hepatitis and was in the hospital for three weeks. She couldn't have coke and several treats and she was really good about it. Well, she finally got over her problems and stayed well. She had her tonsils out after she graduated from high school. To this day, she is still accident prone. Poor kid! Ha! Well, today she is a grandmother and a very loving and caring one.

DAVID MCCAMLY

I am sorry I didn't mention your father and Grandpa in a very good light in some places of my story.

I really don't know a whole lot of his younger life, but will write whatever I can remember.

David's father's name was Francis Pierre McCamly. His mother's name was Mattie Barrett. To this union there were two girls, Eldora and Olive, and then David. When David was three years old, he fell through a hay hole in the hay loft and broke his leg. About the same time of the year, his mother Mattie was shot in an accident. It didn't kill her but she suffered from infection. Getting to a doctor in those days wasn't easy. She was taken to her parents home for care and not at home when David broke his leg. She passed away when David was only three years old.

Granddad McCamly lived with his mother on the McCamly farm which he inherited as his father William was deceased. Granddad's brother Rupert, wife Blanche, and family came there to live for a while to help great Grandma and Granddad raise the children. Then Uncle Dave, Granddad's other brother and wife Rachel came to help after Rupert and Blanche moved elsewhere. Granddad was known as Pierre or Pete. He remarried Anna Dillon and she gave birth to

"Me Laala"

Ivah, known mostly as "Babe" Anne. Granddad Pierre never ever took another lady out to a dance or dinner. He had one sister, Ethel Marie. She married Alfred Hayes. He also had a brother William who was shot crawling through a fence to go rabbit hunting. He was found dead a short distance from fence. The McCamly's originated in Scotland and Ireland and migrated to the United States. Way back in years, a cousin was a General George McCamly in the United States Army.

On the Barrett side was Al Barrett and his daughter, Mattie. She was born in Denmark. Al Barrett was a short, chubby man. He was bald-headed and for many years he was the Clerk of Courts in Gettysburg, It was quite a large family. I'll try to remember all the names. David's uncles were Ed, Percy, Robert and Bud. Percy was killed in World War I. His aunts were Ethel, Alpha and Nellie. Alpha was nicknamed "Sis".

Ed, Percy, and Bud never married. Robert had about five children I believe. Their names were Zella, Lucille, Willard, Dale, and another younger girl whose name I can't remember. I went to high school with Zella, Lucille, and Willard. Ethel and Sis married brothers. Ethel married Kit Brokaw and they had only two children, a boy and a girl. Sis married Jay Brokaw and they had three girls and twin boys. The girls were Nellie, Doris, Jackie. The boys were named Ray and Jay.

David hadn't seen any of his cousins in years. At a young age, in his teens' of early twenty's, he had a terrible crush on his cousin Charlotte, but then they moved to California and he only saw her a few more times. He saw Uncle Jay's and Aunt Sis' kids when Sis passed away. He saw Charlotte again in 1975 in Salinas, California and she was not friendly and no longer a good-looking woman. He was quite taken aback that she hardly acknowledged him. People can change when they get older.

Other than David's broken leg when he was a kid, I don't really know too many interesting events of his childhood. His dad had him living at home and helping some but times were bad during the "Dirty Thirties" as they were called. He went to another town down by Mitchell, South Dakota and worked during harvest time. He also worked a short time for CCC, a government program. He worked in the program 1938 or 1939, just as Social Security was started. He also worked for Everett Money at Onida driving a truck and halling hay. They sold the hay to farmers as none was raised due to no rain. He was paid a little each week for gas for his car, and of course some beer and liquor. He didn't keep track of the hours he worked so when Everett Money didn't need him anymore he wouldn't pay him anything. In later years when Mr. Money passed away and we were already married, he tried to collect his pay from the Money Estate but his daughter also refused to pay him. They had money to pay David, but refused. While working for Mr. Money, he stayed with his cousin Alfred. Alfred's wife Marvel was not the most intelligent person and after the children grew up, Marvel divorced Alfred and she moved to Sioux City, Iowa where their three sons and daughter moved to. Alfred married Zola in Newcastle, Wyoming and four more children were born. Their names were Rachel, Rhonda, Billie, and Jackie. They raised them in Newcastle. The youngest one was still home when they moved to Hills City in the Black Hills. Later they moved to Rapid City, South Dakota.

David was hanging out with his cousin Charles and helping the farmers at harvest time. He became ill and was hospitalized with double dust pneumonia. When Saturday came, he walked out of the hospital but was still so weak. He said he nearly passed out in his car. He stopped at the liquor store and proceeded to celebrate that night partying. He also was seeing a married woman in Onida, Anne Lomheim. Her husband was a trucker and out of town quite a lot. He slept with Anne even though she was pregnant at the time. Well, I guess he got really acquainted too late as she had a family. Hank Lomheim divorced Anne but David wasn't in luck. Anne was also married to another man, Whitey Lemmel while married to Hank. Her youngest daughter with Hank was physically challenged and in a wheelchair all her life.

David's sister Eldora married Joe Tobin. To this union there were five boys and seven girls. Their oldest son, Richard, got spinal

"Me Laala"

meningitis at a young age and passed away. Anne Lomheim was Joe's sister. There were fourteen in Joe's family. All lived to be quite elderly.

Joe and Eldora's twin girls were named after the two Grandmothers, Mary and Mattie. They are both short and chunky like Eldora. They have acquired back problems like osteoporosis and they waddle like a duck when they walk. Of David's nieces and nephews on the Tobin side, four of them have passed away. Olive was between Eldora and David. She went through high school and became a teacher. She also could play the piano. Now, she is a very sweet and sophisticated lady. I don't believe she was a drinker at all. She married Wilbur Christopher and they moved to Coeur d'alene, Idaho. Wilbur worked for a Texaco gas station and then borrowed money and then bought the station. At a later time in her life she became pregnant and had one son, Jerry. Later they moved to Auburn, Washington where they opened up a Coast to Coast hardware store. Olive worked in the store. David never did care for Wilbur. After Jerry had married and moved away, they sold the hardware store in Auburn and moved to California and helped Coast to Coast get a store into a better profitable state. Then they moved to Escondido, California. They came to Las Vegas after David passed away for his funeral and were in a terrible accident. They were with Wilbur's brother-in-law at the time. They were both injured.

In later years, Wilbur passed away in a care center in Washington. Olive went to the dining room to get Wilbur's lunch for him and when she came back, Wilbur had passed away. The last letter I had from her she said she would like to see me one more time. I am afraid she will have to be satisfied with a letter from me with her birthday card.

Ivah or "Babe" married William Campbell in 1939. She was seventeen and nineteen years younger than Bill. Bill inherited the ranch and oil royalties from his father who had moved to Texas. Babe spent money for many years like it would last forever. She was even put in jail for bad checks after they lost the ranch. She passed away after we came to Las Vegas. Bill passed away several years before that. They had three sons, Billy, Colin, and Arlo.

When David was in grade school, he had a kid's crush on Mary Ellen Collins. He thought she was the most beautiful girl. The Collins family lived not too far from them in Sully County, South Dakota. My family lived in Potter County, about seventeen miles north of Gettysburg and they lived twenty miles south. Well, the Collins moved north of Gettysburg and we met them. Walter, Dorthy, and I went to grade school with Wayne and Glen Collins. Walter went to high school with Mary Ellen. David lost track of the beautiful Mary Ellen. He used to say that Mary Ellen was his first girlfriend. When he became about sixteen, his crush was on his cousin, Charlotte.

When David was twenty-one, he told his sister Olive that he would never marry. Well, when he was twenty-six, we were married. Olive reminded him about that statement.

There was this one incident where his aunt used to kid him about when he was about eleven years old, his Aunt Rachel, who was living with Great Granddad to help with raising the four children say, "One night I heard someone up and there was David standing by the window where all the beautiful geranium house plants were. It was moonlight out and there was no indoor bathroom and David had to go." She asked him how come he didn't go outside and he said, "The plant was thirsty."

David's aunt and uncle Hayes lived a half a mile south of them and he would walk or run there if he got into trouble. Aunt Ethel knew he had been up to mischief when David came in all out of breath. He used to spend time there with his cousin Frankie while his dad and great grandma or whoever was there helping, went to town. His uncle Al had diabetes and they tried to keep sweets from him, but the kids would find food hid in a building. Well, Uncle Al lost his arm a few inches below the shoulder from the diabetes. They sold the farm and moved to Coeur d'alene, Idaho, where Aunt Ethel ran a rooming house. Board and room made them a good living even when it was cheap.

I'll now try to continue this story. Great Grandma McCamly was still alive when I met David. I met her one time as David took me to visit her one weekend. She was a small lady and quite frail when I met her. She passed away a few months after that.

One Saturday night in Gettysburg, my girlfriend June Wickart said "Come on girls we are going to Onida to the dance." She was talking to Dorothy, my cousin Doris Packard, and I. It was David, his friends Frank and Charlie Tobin, and cousin Charles McCamly we were riding with. Oh yes, and David's then girlfriend. So there were nine of us in David's car. When we got to the dance we all went in but David, as he didn't dance. After a while, I went out to the car and David and I got acquainted. Nothing unusual went on, of course. We just visited. After he got off to work at Schlackter lumber he drove up and down Main Street, which was the going entertainment in those days and Dorothy and I were on our way from high school. David drove by and pulled up to the curb and waited for us. We talked some more and he took us home to Grandma Johnson's where we were staying. This came to be an everyday occurrence. Soon he dropped his girlfriend Minnie Riector, who had a baby out of wedlock when he met her. So she wasn't respected at all because of her child. Things are different today. Back then, girls were condemned for giving birth and not married but the man that had a hand in making that child was not condemned for abandoning the girl. Having a child did not cool her sexual desires. He was lucky she never got pregnant. She left Gettysburg and moved to California. We then started our relationship. We had only one breakup and that was with June Norris. He came back to me as soon as she started to talk about marriage.

David worked in the Gettysburg area most of the time until his dad needed him to help on the farm. Then I would only see him maybe on Wednesday and Saturday. He was never mean or used any foul words to me until years after we were married and then only a couple of times. Then he would be embarrassed and wouldn't talk to me for a week. I wouldn't know why he would not talk to me. Anyway, I'm ahead of myself again. This is easy to do since so much has happened in my life. David drank a lot and he staggered down the street one Saturday night. I was sitting in the car with Mom and Dad and even though they were against drinking, they got a kick out of watching David rub his hand along the window of Moore's Hardware Store. David was about the only man that was allowed to come and get me. I never could understand that beings they didn't drink. I guess they wanted to get me married off and they wouldn't have to feed and clothe me.

Our neighbor and second cousin came and picked me up but one date with him was enough for me. Although they weren't hurting for money, I would have been financially secure.

I met David in February of 1939 and he told me a year later that it was marry him soon or not at all. Well, I became pregnant about that time so we planned our wedding for April 19, 1940. We nearly weren't married that afternoon as the minister didn't get my letter until late in the forenoon, as the mailman had dropped it in the gutter a block from his house. A neighbor boy found it and took it to him. David went to Lebanon to the minister's house that afternoon on his way out to our place. We were married in the living room or I should say, we had a parlor wedding. My brother Walter and wife, Minnie, were our attendants. Mom fixed a nice dinner and the minister, Reverend Krueger, stayed and dined with us. We may not have gotten married but good fortune was with us. When David was on his way out to our place, he came barreling down the gravel road going ninety miles an hour. He had his dad's new 1939 Chevrolet with twin horns. There, as he came down this big hill, was someone's herd of horses on the middle of the bridge. He had no way to stop at that speed so he laid on the twin horns and the horses split and he went between them. He didn't hit any of them. I doubt if it even stopped him from driving so fast as he was already late getting there. He came and got me and we went into town and picked out his suit. I waited fifteen minutes for them to hem the pants and got back out the seventeen miles in time to dress for the five o'clock evening wedding. I made a mad dash for the bathroom, which was outside and tripped and fell down. Sometimes I don't think we were meant to get married that day. After dinner and Reverend Krueger had left, we went up to the Stuckes, our neighbors, and the men played pinochle. That was the extent of our honeymoon. We got home to David's at about two thirty in the morning. So we were still in bed at two o'clock in the afternoon, when Granddad McCamly came to our room and said, "Aren't you going to get up today? David, there are two flat tires on the car." So we got up. They took the tires off and took them to town and had to get one new one and fix the other.

David helped his dad in the field and milking the cows. I took over the chickens and made a big garden. When he was in the field close enough to the house, I'd take him a sandwich and something cold to drink. We had an old radio but that's all the entertainment for a young sixteen year old wife all week long. I made baby clothes and after Vonnie was born, I had all the diapers and baby things. I would wash everything by hand most of the time. We had to heat the wash water on the stove and wash in the entry way as the washing machine had a gas engine and the exhaust had to be piped out the door. After Vonnie was old enough to take outside and down to the corral, I learned to help milk the cows. Vonnie would sit on a blanket and the dog laid beside her while we did the milking. They were Granddad McCamly's cows but the cream that was sold bought the groceries. So, it was a necessity that the cows be milked when Granddad McCamly went to town and didn't come home until midnight or so. I felt sorry for David, working in the field all day and then had to come in and milk a dozen or so cows. Well, that started me doing a lot of the cow milking.

THROUGH THE YEARS WITH DAVID

*I*n 1940 we had no income. Sometimes Granddad Pierre McCamly would give us money to go to the movie on Saturday night. Sometimes there would be a house party at someone's house. Granddad always bought liquor when we went to parties. Sometimes there were dances at Copp School or the school David had gone years before. I was gardening and making baby clothes and even quilts as there were plenty of scrap material from Great Grandma McCamly. I never had any help with the washing and cooking. I guess we were trained from childhood to know how to do these things. Vonnie was born and we changed milk on her and she cried most of the time for two nights and two days. David had to give me a break and get up part of the night and hold and rock her. Life on the farm was not easy.

In 1941 David helped the neighbors and bought a 1929 car as he had sold the 1931 Chevy to Walter. We remained not having any money. We cleaned South Lowell School House to have a little money to buy a few necessary baby goodies. I had a miscarriage in August of 1941. It was a baby boy who lived eleven hours. We named him Francis Alvin. He is buried at Appromatich Cemetery northwest of Gettysburg. Granddad made the coffin and Francis was buried next to my baby sister Martha Luann who died also thirty days old from whooping cough and pneumonia. Our neighbor, Ms. Hanson, delivered Francis Alvin. We had the doctor come but he didn't take the baby to Pierre, South Dakota to the hospital to be put in an incubator. My dad fixed a light for heat in the bassinet and they used hot water bottles but he still didn't make it. I guess it wasn't meant to be. God took him to Heaven.

In 1942, I recalled that we got an FHA loan and purchased some sheep and hogs. The hogs got out one day and David took the saddle horse and rounded them up but beings it was Spring and the top of the ground was slippery as the frost was coming out. The horse fell and broke David's leg. He was taken to the doctor in Gettysburg and then up to my folks for a couple of days until he wasn't in so much pain. Vonnie and I went up and stayed too. We now were property owners and made it more important to be home. We traded our '29 car off for a '38 Dodge. Some neighbors about six miles away lost their sheep and when we get a different car, Grace accused us of stealing their sheep and selling them to buy this car. Several years later, they bought that car as we had traded it in by then. In 1943, life was about the same except Vonnie got the whooping cough. We left her at the neighbors on a Saturday when we went to town so she wouldn't be exposed to it, but the neighbor's son was the first to get it and so Vonnie got it too. Sharon was born on Granddad McCamly's birthday. Vonnie was in a room at Mom and Dad's that had been Great Grandma Bartels' homestead shack. My Dad, brother, cousin, daughter, and nephew were all born in that room. Great Grandpa Bartels had built onto that room and the house ended up to be a three story, fifteen room house. Sharon was born in the kitchen at Mom and Dad's. David wouldn't sleep in the same room as Vonnie and I because he couldn't stand to hear her whoop like that.

In 1944, David and Granddad McCamly got into many arguments so when my mom and dad decided to go to Lawrence, Kansas and work in the powder plant, we moved to their farm and share-cropped with David and Walter. At least it was a living. We had our hogs and sheep, milk and eggs so life really wasn't all that bad. Walter drank a lot and things weren't too good all the time. In 1945, we were at the farm until after Ethel was born when Granddad McCamly sold the

McCamly farm and bought one six miles from my folks and then David agreed to move back to be with his dad. My mom and dad had come back from Kansas and we would have to find a place to move to so we moved down where the kids will remember as their home. In 1946, we now had three children as Ethel was born on Vonnie's birthday and one day before David's. The house we lived in was the oldest still standing in the area except for a few others. We traded cars again and bought a 1941 Ford coupe from Dick Hall. We took the space behind the seat and the men made a seat in the back for the kids. We had that car for quite a few years.

It is 1947 and still work, work, work. We had bought some milk cows by then so we had grocery and gas money and of course David and his father were drinking a lot. They went to town one day with a truck load of grain and sold that, then went to the pool hall and drank too much beer. When leaving town, David failed to stop at a stop sign and was given a warning to get out of town. Well, this made him mad so he went back to town with his father and they were put in jail. The sheriff called me to let me know. This made me mad and I said to myself, "I'm not going to milk all those cows alone again," and I didn't. The next morning I didn't even make breakfast. I took the three girls and went to the jail and said, "Give me some money so we can eat and the cows aren't milked." David said "Don't get so smart and mouthy." Well, I said "Your sister Olive is coming today. Aren't you ashamed. She'll come and Brother and Father will be in jail." She and son Jerry got to town before they got home. When David and his father got home, they were like two kids that had been naughty. I was expecting Terry and a few months before he was born, David and his father were in town. David was racing home and ran into a ditch. Wayne Worth brought him home. He thought I had called and told him I was having labor pains but I hadn't called. I was fine. Wayne took us back to the car and I drove it out of the ditch and drove home. David got a black eye was all. He had left his dad in town so as soon as we got the chores done, we had to go back to town and pick up Granddad McCamly. They then got in an argument and they wouldn't talk to each other for three or four days. David would tell me to go tell his dad this or that and his dad would say to tell David this and that. That happened quite a few times in the years. Terry was born November 1st. I went to a lady in town to have him. My brother-in-law Jim, called David up as he had gone back home to milk the cows. Jim told David he had a son. David called him a liar, but he found out Jim wasn't lying. Mary Ruth and Jim lived in town so Mary Ruth helped keep the three girls. Not much happened in 1948. On the fourth of July, Darleen Tobin came out and stayed with the kids and David and I went to Mobridge to the rodeo. Dorothy, Jim, Granddad McCamly, David, Mary Tobin, and I all went. Of course they were all drinking. Mary wasn't very old, about fourteen, and they gave her all the mixed drinks she could drink. Mary was drunk and sick by the time we got to the rodeo. They all went in a bar and walked Mary around to sober her up. Our friends, Ben and Gen Shoup and their kids were there. I was with Gen and the kids as Ben went where the rest of the gang was. Well, you might know that I was accused of being somewhere with Ben. We never got to the rodeo. They were all so drunk I had to drive home about midnight. It was about forty miles home. They were still drinking in the car. Dorothy and Jim got into an argument and David and his dad got into one. I had to stop so they could get out and fight, but before they hit each other, they realized they were Father and Son. David's dad came to the barnyard when Jim and I were milking the cows in the dark and wanted to know what was going on down there. I was accused of wrong doing. I wished sometimes someone cared enough for me to take me away. It was November 18, 1948 when David quit drinking. Never did drink anymore which made life a little better.

Dixie was born in 1949 the day after Granddad's birthday. David was so afraid I might have her at home or we would get caught in a storm on the way to the doctor in Onida so I stayed in Onida for about two weeks before she was born. Dixie was born about five days early, otherwise she would have been born on my brother's birthday.

David and his dad went to town every Saturday. I was not away from home for six weeks in the winter. Dixie had pneumonia when she was a month old. She had infected eczema when she was six months old. A coffee burn, which was Vonnie's and my fault as David said Vonnie should have been home instead of spending a week at the Shoup's. Of course, again, he made me cry with his accusations. Although David was jealous as all get out, he did not consider my feelings.

In 1950, we needed to borrow more money to continue farming. We bought our first new car. It was a 1950 light blue Studebaker. It had real good gas mileage and was big enough for our family. I can't recall if the kids had any mishaps except that Terry had a pull out fracture of his arm.

In 1951, Vonnie, Sharon, and Ethel were in the hospital together and had their tonsils out. We had health insurance by that time. I recall the doctor bill for when Vonnie was born was twenty five dollars. Dr Burgess never did get paid. Dr. Siegel charged thirty five dollars and was paid when Sharon was born. He was the doctor when Ethel was born. His bill was fifty dollars. Dr. Collins was the doctor when Terry was born and that was seventy dollars to him and ten dollars to the midwife, Mrs. Dutt. When Dixie was born, Dr. Hale, who was a chiropractor and baby doctor, charged one hundred and twenty-five dollars. Dixie was in December and in February I had a partial hysterectomy. Arlene Jager and her kids came and helped David take care of the kids and she also knew how to milk cows. She was a big help. She stayed a couple of days after I got home. A week after I got home, I washed clothes and hung them on the line outside in the cold twenty degrees below zero. I helped milk the cows. Maybe that was why I never got good enough to have had pain and blood clots during menstruation.

In 1952, Dixie got burned from a cup of coffee. Her little fingers pulled the cup off the cupboard onto her. We never had coffee at night but David was going out to the field and plow until midnight as many of the farmers did as crop planting got a late start due to too much rain early. The tractor had lights by then. Well, he didn't get to the field that night. I was afraid at first to tell him what had happened as he would blame me for not setting my cup back farther. He blamed me and Vonnie. As he said if Vonnie had been home instead of spending a week at Ben Shoup's she could have been watching her. That wasn't fair of him at all.

Moving along, in 1952 I started plowing, discing, drilling, harrowing, and then helping put up the hay as Granddad McCamly could not work in the field in the Spring as he had an appendicitis operation and couldn't drive the tractor for a while. I would milk the cows after coming in from the field. While David separated the milk, fed the calves and pigs, I gathered the eggs and cooked dinner. It would be nine or ten o'clock before Vonnie and I would finish the dishes.

In 1953, I only remember a small amount of this year that wasn't routine. There was everyday farm work. If there was a blizzard we would be milking early and eat pancakes then play pinochle. That was always the routine if there was a blizzard. Granddad McCamly bought a new car so we bought his old car from him. He couldn't stand to have us have a newer car than he.

Another year of hard work in 1954. David never got any faster with getting up to do the chores or get into the field and get the crops in on time. He was always the last to get the crop planted, last to harvest, and last to get the hall in. There just was no hurry to him but everything was done to perfection. He would not get out to the barn until I'd have two or three cows already milked.

Bad year for crops again in 1955. Hail storm took quite a toll on our corn crop. Some of our late wheat crop survived the hail. The corn crop did survive the hail storm. We started moving hay six miles from home and out across the river on Indian land. That is when David lost his Black Hills gold wedding band, which I was able to pay for by saving enough egg money. While moving hay across the river we came upon a rattlesnake. David wouldn't even run over it with the tractor wheel because it would come up the tire and strike him. He threw wrenches at it until it came out of the horse hoof track and slithered away. I can't remember any outstanding happenings in 1956. I do recall David going on an overnight fishing trip with Lon McClure just when we had a small heifer to have a calf. My orders were to go out at midnight and three o'clock in the morning to check on her. This was very upsetting to me as he didn't worry enough about the heifer to postpone going fishing. David really didn't care to fish but Lon went a lot, so he didn't have to go at that particular time, but he did.

The year of 1957 was a bad year. There were six accidents within a six mile radius from May through November. Not all were car accidents. The first one was a neighbor boy that tipped the tractor over and it killed him. The second was a neighbor boy, who at the age of eleven, rolled the pickup and got killed. The third accident occurred when my parents home exploded from a butane gas leak. Mom, Mary Ruth, Jim, and Carla were all hospitalized. That was the fifteen room house that my grandfather built. My dad used what lumber he could salvage and built a smaller more modern home but still put in a gas butane heater. The fourth was Vonnie's car accident. She dropped a pencil on the floor and instead of waiting until she got to school, she tried to pick it up and lost control of the car. A neighbor boy came and told us and David just walked out, got in the pickup and went to the accident without even telling me. The neighbor boy hadn't left when I stepped out and he told me. I don't know if David would have even called me. Vonnie had just paid her insurance with the school the day before her accident. The doctor gave us no hope for four days. Two men from the Radar Military Base donated and so did Coe Frankhouser, the attorney. We went to Radar Base after the insurance paid for the donors. The fifth involved Ralph Schutterle, who was up in his years. He had an appendicitis operation. The appendix burst just as they were taking it out. He had quite a time recuperating. The next accident happened when Ronnie Tanner's, a neighbor, saddle horse fell and the saddle horn punctured his stomach. He was not killed.

It was January 1957 that a near tragedy occurred at our farm. It was cold and we didn't have two ten power. We had thirty-two volt batteries charged by a motor. This unit was in a storm cellar or basement just south of the house. Just a hole in the dirt. David started the motor to charge up the batteries. The exhaust pipe was extended just out of the cellar. Not knowing the pipe had frozen over, the exhaust went under the house, which came up inside. Dixie was the smallest and she started falling down which alerted Granddad McCamly that we were breathing in the fumes. David was working outside so didn't get any fumes but came in the house and found out. He started to get the kids parkas on and get them outside. First he went and found the pipe frozen and shut the motor off. Sharon went outside and the cold air hit her and she fell to the ground. We all somehow made it out. We opened up the house to let it air out. Vonnie was staying in town as she was in high school. I went outside to go to the barn to milk the cows and when the cold air hit me, I just slid down the wall. David helped me up and we went on with the chores. By 1960 we were able to get two ten power and a television. A sad occurrence turned out with no one hurt. We just had headaches for a few hours. Life is very challenging and you never know when or where it is coming from.

We sold our farm on March 21, 1962. In April 1962 we headed out to Montana, Idaho, Washington, then Oregon. We looked for my cousin in Oregon, but no luck. We journeyed on down to Staton, Oregon to visit Norbert and Irene Frost and spent two days there with them. Irene was Joe Tobin's niece. They were both raised in Potter County.

On to Yukaipa, California to someone David had known and then to Vallejo to visit the Murphys. David had gone to grade school with their boys. Also, in Vallejo was one of David's teacher, Christina. Christina was a cousin to Uncle Jim Wilcox. We spent a day and night with them.

We traveled down Pacific Highway One and could see the ocean every once in a while. We visited David's Aunt Ethel and Uncle Kit Brokaw. He was quite shocked at the ramshackle apartment they lived in. Both were heavy beer drinkers and quite a disappointment to David.

We then went to San Diego and stayed with Aunt Sis and Uncle Jay Brokaw. Uncle Jay thought he'd get me lost, but I was driving and went right back to their house. Uncle Jay took me to Tijuana and David turned down the wrong way on a one way street. A man stepped out of his car and held up the traffic so we could turn around. Uncle Jay thought it was funny and laughed and laughed about it. It was a little scary to us farmers. We spent a couple of days there and came to Las Vegas. It was a two lane highway at that time. We were going along near Victorville and off to the West was a Joshua tree forest.

We arrived at Dorothy and Jim Brokaw's and spent two weeks there. David did not look in the paper for job opportunities but I did. I found my job at Southern Nevada Telephone Company who soon changed its name to Central Telephone. David wanted to fly back to South Dakota for Terry's eighth grade graduation but I said, "No. We will be going after the kids in a week anyway." He held that in his mind for a long time and resented the fact that I wouldn't go.

We left to get Ethel, Terry, and Dixie and what things we hadn't sold. We had to buy a pickup truck to haul everything back to Las Vegas. We left South Dakota with an old used Studebaker pickup and our new Chevy. We went to Newcastle, Wyoming and spent the night at Alfred and Zola's. Something broke on the pickup so we never left until in the afternoon, so we stayed in Casper, Wyoming that night. Then on to Cedar City, Utah that night. We had run short of cash and David had an awful time cashing a traveler's check as a bunch had been stolen and were cashed between Alaska and California. Finally, a bar cashed one, a fifty dollar check, and we got a motel and dinner. It was the first time we felt like we could afford a nice dinner. The girls wanted to get a tuna sandwich but David made them order something better and it made Dixie sick. Now we are about to our new home in Las Vegas, Nevada. Dorothy and Jim bought a house for us to rent. On Monday, we went and bought furniture and moved in. So on Wednesday, I went to the phone company and put in my application and started that day at four thirty in the afternoon.

In July, Vonnie and Sharon came to Las Vegas. Vonnie went back to Wyoming to work. Sharon and Wayne, her husband, were with us in Las Vegas until November when they went back to South Dakota. They moved to Montana and lived there for years. While they were with us, we took off and drove to Reno. I didn't realize Reno was so far. I had Saturday and Sunday off so we had to get back Sunday night. David didn't do much looking for work for two months. Vonnie and Al, her husband, came back and worked here in Las Vegas. Al went to work at Mission Linen where David was working and Vonnie went to work at Kresge Department Store.

Tom Mienan, a friend, and I were delivering Avon in 1962 and while on a delivery, I fell off of the step onto the cement drive and broke my hip. We completed the deliveries and I was in a lot of pain. I was alright as long as I didn't move too much. When we finished delivering, Tom took me to the emergency room and it was confirmed that my hip was broken. I had surgery and three screws were placed in my hip. I recovered from that pretty well.

Sometime between 1963 to 1964, Vonnie and Al moved to California and after a few years, Sharon and Wayne did too. David got so he hated sorting clothes at Mission Linen and decided to put in his application with the city. Mission Linen found out he had applied with the city so they fired him in August just short of three years. He wasn't hired by the city until October. By this time we had bought a house that was two years old. So, even though the payments were only a hundred and nine dollars a month, my pay wasn't very much. I started at a dollar and thirty five cents an hour and probably was earning a dollar fifty by then as the union got us raises. David drew unemployment for three months and then when they learned that Terry was working at Mission Linen, they made David pay allowances for Terry back. Terry was going to school and working. He had to buy gas for his car and personal spending money but they still required David to pay back two hundred and thirty dollars. David started with the city and worked at Woodlawn Cemetery for thirteen years. They deducted some time due to David injuring his back on the job. He and his friend, Virgil Qualls, were handling the heavy cement vaults when he hurt his back.

Lots of years passed between 1966 and 1987. We made several trips a year back to South Dakota. Quite a number of our relatives passed away and we tried to attend as many funerals and family gatherings as possible. In that period of time we had traded cars quite a few times. The first one we purchased in Las Vegas was a 1959 Chevy Impala. Vonnie and Al bought that from us. I believe the next car we bought was a 1970 Monte Carlo. Then in 1972 we bought an Omega Oldsmobile then in 1975 another Chevrolet Impala. In 1979 we got a 1979 Buick, then in 1981 a Chevrolet diesel. We changed to Ford in 1985 and David's last car was a 1987 Thunderbird. He had always wanted a Thunderbird and why he didn't have one before that is hard to understand.

In 1986 David became ill with cancer and was hospitalized for fifty-five days. He regained his health and I retired from Central Telephone. When we were on our six weeks trip through all the states we hadn't been in, David began to have trouble breathing. It really wasn't a very enjoyable trip as he didn't want to stop where he would need to do any walking. So, all I about saw were trees and highways. I drove nine thousand of the ninety-five hundred miles we drove. He did enjoy Mackinaw Island, Michigan. He wanted to go to Atlantic City, New Jersey, but didn't tell me until we were passed the highway to go there and I refused to go back. I wanted to go to the Statue of Liberty, Freedom Trail in Boston, all of Philadelphia, and Washington, DC but David wouldn't read the map to tell me where we had to go. We saw something off the highway but what can you see when driving seventy miles an hour?

We got back to Gettysburg in time to go to Ralph and Lois Shoup's fiftieth wedding anniversary. I think he enjoyed that the most of all our trip. In December 1987 the doctor told David his cancer had come back. In January 1988 he started chemotherapy. Five different types of chemo were used but to no avail. I have always felt that if the doctor had removed the affected lung, David may have lived quite a few years longer. I thought that the doctor had told him he had about six months left but he hadn't and when I was on the phone telling Dixie the results, he turned around in his chair and said, "What was that you said?" So, I had to tell him. When he had to start having chemo he just gave up and wouldn't even try to get better. One's frame of mind is part of the healing process.

David left us in 1988. One good thing was he never suffered in pain like many people do. We can and know when the end is coming but we are never ready for it. Of all the vehicles I mentioned, we had a Nash convertible that we got from Carla after she and Terry were married. David had a Volkswagon Beetle. We drove that a lot. It was a good little car. We made a couple of trips to South Dakota with it.

David had a good heart but was a jealous person and he did have a temper. When he couldn't control his anger, he took it out on me, which, in later years, wasn't very often. He was good about buying me clothes and things. After he retired he did get to gambling some. He liked to play Keno and at one time, there were double machines. He played nickel double machines for hours at the Hilton. He liked the dime machines and finally got to playing quarter Joker's wild machines at the Sundance Casino.

I don't know if he thought I was going to sit at home after he was gone, but he told Al he was afraid I'd fine another man. Well, I did, but never wanted to marry again or have that close a relationship. I'm my own person, enjoy other people and good times I didn't have when a teenager. David is on my mind much more than most people think. You might say that I grew up with him. For forty-eight years he was my shoulder to lean on.

We invested and saved but it was mostly my money that was invested and David paid for the basic living expenses. He would turn over in his grave if he knew I had blown it all. Terry always said, "Mom, it's your money. Enjoy it. Don't feel you have to save it for us kids." Guess I didn't but no one, I hope, can take away the twenty thousand life insurance.

It seems odd that we never had life insurance on David. His city pension wasn't put in for me to continue getting half of it at least. Nothing in finances was given to me as far as retirement assistance.

I remember a young telephone operator, Denise, who became ill with cancer. I think David met her once. She was a very pretty girl and she had a cute little boy. Well, Denise's husband divorced when he found out she had cancer. This made David so mad. If he could have done something to Denise's husband, I think he would have. Denise was buried at Woodlawn and David made sure the grave was taken care of. Her husband was not a good man. He wouldn't even let her mother see her only grandson anymore. David was very soft-hearted about those kinds of things.

I guess that about wraps up my story about David. Every time my roses are beautiful and I get ready to take a bouquet out to the cemetery, the wind comes up bad so there is no use taking them.

Another thing David always wanted was to go back to South Dakota for memorial to decorate the graves on both sides of the family. A little costly to buy all those flowers. Charlotte Packard, my cousin's wife took care of them when we weren't there, but she passed away from cancer later. I have no idea who cares for the graves now, but I imagine my nephew, Richard Bartels, and wife, Sandra, are taking care of Mom and Dad's. For the McCamlys in Onida, probably no one takes care of the graves or provides flowers. Ivah's son, Colin and wife, Janet, did take care of them for a while, but have moved to Rapid City and may not go back there every year.

This pretty much covers the most important details of our lives.

MERRY CHRISTMAS 2008

Quite a few things have happened since I wrote my story. Time goes so fast. I guess it's about seven years ago. I had a car accident on August 25, 2000 and fractured my hip so no bowling that winter. I did start in January and finished out the season, but by the time the bowling league ended, my hip was hurting a lot so in June 2001 the screws had to be replaced with shorter ones. It wasn't a big deal. Dixie came up when I had the surgery and she told the nurse at the desk she wanted the screws that were removed because her husband was building a new deck. That made them laugh. When the winter leagues started up again I was back to bowling, but have never gotten back to my 160 average. Averaging 146 is about the tops.

Life just stayed about the same old grind, clean house, gardening some and did my own yard work. Tom Mienan, a close friend who lived with me, was working for the Review Journal and I stayed on at the bridal shop until it closed in 2004. I really didn't miss staying home as I accomplished quite a bit. Ethel was living with me and Delvin, her son, was too.

I was delivering Avon with Tom. He was raised on a farm so I thought he would make a good man. Found out he wasn't as I thought.

I decided 5 years ago to go back to South Dakota for the Hanson-Johnson reunion. Dixie and Ethel went with me. Pam was on the schedule to have Ethel's grandchild. We left on Thursday morning and had breakfast in St. George, Utah then made it to Rawlins, Wyoming about five o'clock in the evening. We got a room, went and got some dinner and back to the motel. I checked back on how Pam was doing and Danielle was very close to being born. About an hour later she popped out into this world. What a doll!

We left Rawlins the next morning and got to Matt and Laura's in Hot Springs, South Dakota early in the day. That was Friday. Saturday we stayed and Matt took us for a drive to Deadwood going through Custer State Park. While there, we saw a herd of buffalo up close.

On Sunday we all went to Gettysburg to the reunion. We also visited my parents' graves and many other relative's graves. We went to Onida to Granddad McCamly's grave and other relatives as well. We got to say "hello" to our old friends, Jim Shoup and Marge Shoup Zebroski to catch up on the Shoup family news. During our stay in Gettysburg, we visited Aunt Dodie, Mattie, and Neil. They were all in the Oahu Nursing Home. Aunt Dodie knew me, but not Ethel or Dixie. We had a ball talking with her. We also went to the county fair and met up with our old neighbors, the Tanners, Pete, Bea, Ronnie, and Mary. They all looked real good. Of course we had to stop by the Medicine Rock Inn, a restaurant well known in those parts. We ran into a few business acquaintances and friends while having coffee.

Matt's two littlest ones came back with us. Josiah wasn't too happy about it, but Matt and Laura were taking a bus of church kids to Minneapolis for a convention. Josiah and Shandy were to stay with Dixie and Duane for two weeks but guess they had to take them home after one week. That is the last time I have been back home. My Nephew Bobby Dale Wilcox passed away from cancer. He loved his beer drinking, smoking, and going to bars. His wife said he was a lot of fun when he was drunk. He was gone from this earth two weeks before Dorothy and Jim even told me. They had him cremated and his wife has his ashes. We never see or hear from her.

I continued doing courier service with Tom. He was getting dementia and couldn't find his way home, but he never forgot our phone number and would call me and tell me what street he was on.

I would then tell him how to get home. I got better about telling him to turn right or left. He sometimes went right passed here. It was an experience! He would then go get his deliveries and was still able to put them in the order that he would go. I would have to guide him back home to pick me up to help him make deliveries. The last month he worked I had to take the deliveries in and watch and guide him to the next stop. After he retired, I left him home so I could go play bunco. He would go to the Western to gamble. He found his way there but got lost coming home. Beings I wasn't home, Pat, who rented a room from me, heard the phone ring and figured out where he was. He had a flat tire, so Pat changed it and got him home. That was the last time Tom drove a car. Tom continued to get worse, falling a lot and I couldn't get him up by myself. Delvin helped him get back into the transport chair several times. I finally called the paramedics and he was taken to the Henderson Health Care Center. That is where he remained. He thought that I was his mother and that Ethel was his sister. When Tom passed on April 10, 2010. I sold his car and paid for his cremation. Dorthy, my sister, was put in the Manor Nursing Home. Bonnie Mae, her daughter, came and wrote out the bills for Jim. She tried to take her mom and dad into her home, but that only lasted two weeks. Jim, who was cantankerous had to cause trouble. So, back to their home for Jim, and back to theManor for Dorthy. I took over writing Jim's bills and taking him for medical appointments. Billie, who was Dorthy and Jim's son, died from starvation and liver disease. He hadn't been home for a couple of years. He lived in the desert in a small trailer and had no water, power, and very little food. He made sure his dog got food. I was with Jim and Dorthy when the Lake Mead Hospital called and said Billie had been brought in and died fifteen minutes later. Neither Dorthy nor Jim shed a tear. Jim's worry was getting Billie's trailer out of the desert as he said,"I own that trailer." He was cremated too. I don't know where his ashes are but imagine either with Linda or Danny, his brother or sister. Well, Jim passed away a year ago in September 2007 and Dorthy passed away in September 2008. Danny and Linda cleaned out the place and it was sold for sixty-five thousand dollars. The money went to

Medicare for Dorthy's care. It sat vacant for over a year. A lady bought it and it still was vacant until a couple of months ago.

It has been fifteen months since my heart attack and quadruple bypass surgery. God just isn't ready to take me away yet. I don't have the strength to do a lot, but keep my house reasonably clean. My blood pressure is too low, but maybe they will get that regulated someday.

Pat Gallahan is renting a room at my home and is very good to me and now I have Tom's ex-son-in-law, Jim, living here and he is also good to me. Jim is a long haul driver so he isn't here very much. He pays his rent early and is very neat and clean. He takes me out to eat and to go see Tom when he is here. He also calls me every week or so. Seems like all the trucking is pretty much in the mid-west and central states. Jim is very hyper and can't sit still very long.

Pat has lived with me for fourteen years or more. He makes car and insurance payments. Pat and I went to Laughlin once and spent two days there. We also went to Dixie and Duane's for an afternoon and a night. We went to Armagosa and back to Pahrump and spent the night, just to get out of town for a change. We bowl on Monday night and Tuesday morning. I bowl on Thursday afternoon also. I don't do very good but it's exercise and I enjoy it. I have taken up writing poetry and have about a dozen poems written. Dixie is typing them up for me. I guess I'll never write a book like I've always thought about. I do have one poem published. I didn't know that my nephew, Rick, was poetically inclined and he has two books published. I won't go that far with mine as he said it was costly to have them printed and put in a book.

I am not going to do much sewing anymore and I don't cook a whole lot. I play canasta on Saturdays at a new friend's, Patty Conley. There are four of us and we each take some food and have a big lunch. There are two men against two women. It gives me something to do. Other than bowling, playing cards, bunco, and gambling, which I shouldn't do but you only live once, are what I do. I say my days are numbered.

2009 AND BEYOND

Jerry came home to live with me for a few weeks as his wife Laura told him if he wasn't out in thirty days she would have the cops come and put him out. Well, he went back to Laura's on their anniversary. What a big mistake, but he wanted a mother for his kids, Tracy and Jeana. Laura did things to drive them away. She blamed every thing on them. Tracy left and married and had two girls and a boy. Jeana went to live with Grandma Jean in New Mexico.

Ethel and her husband, Tom, started having trouble and so did Sharon and her husband, Wayne. Both of them divorced about the same time. Ethel bought a nice mobile home. Sharon tried to get by alone but ended up with her daughter, Kathleen. On April 13, 2010, Ethel passed away and six weeks later, Ethel's son, Delvin, left my house and went to a motel and finished his life with alcoholism. Ethel and Delvin both had lived with me so that was a big loss in a few weeks.

Ethel had a hernia in her small intestine and it shut off the blood to the bowel. That caused gangrene to poison her system. I feel like the hospital should have done the exploratory surgery the first day. They had to sedate her with so much pain medication her small body could not handle it. They didn't operate until the fourth day. She passed away that night. Delvin, her oldest son, drank himself to death six weeks after his mother passed. I'll never forget the last words he said to me. I said jokingly, "Now where are you going?" He gave me a dirty look and replied, "You're not my mother." Then he left. Their deaths were so hard to bear that it was hard to keep my sanity.

Patrick Gallahan worked for me delivering Avon and stayed with me after going back to be a bartender. Somehow he continued to stay on and said he loved me and "not as a mother". Of course the age difference kept us apart as a couple. Pat was thirty-one years younger than me. My life in 2010 was a happy life. My family wanted me to sell my mobile home but I didn't then. Patrick's friend, Jim Romanowski, rented a room in the mobile to have a place to stay when he was in town. Jim has been a very good friend ever since.

PATRICK GALLAHAN

Life with Pat just fell into place. I helped Pat as much as possible raising his daughter, Mallory. Mallory's mom was complicated.

He only stayed married to her for three years before coming to live with me. He wrecked my car in 2008 and we traded it in for another in May of 2008. We kept the car in good condition at all times.

In December 2012, I sold my property and moved into a rental home. My one granddaughter, Lisa, moved to Vegas and I helped them with their rent. Pat also gave her rides back to their apartment. I had taken my fuel credit card back from her as they gave me no money and was using it for all kinds of stuff. She called me a bad name but wouldn't tell me what it was. Pat didn't want to ever see her again. Vonnie and her daughters, Lisa and Lori, came up and he stayed in his room most of the time and didn't see Lisa but a few minutes. He wouldn't speak to her.

My bones don't hurt but my muscles do. I can't understand why I feel sleepy. Now I understand why Dorthy always complained when in the nursing home. Although I'm sure they give the patients sleeping pills to keep them quiet and calm. The doctors say none of my pills have a sedative in them.

Most days are about the same. I get up early, listen to the news on television for about an hour. Then I turn to the game shows. I clean the house, fix something to eat for when Pat gets home from work. I clean the kitchen again then watch television then off to bed to read a book. How ever long I can stay awake. I never slept good. I would wake up and look at the clock about every hour. I don't know why I did this, but I don't want to get dependent on a sleep enhancer. Sometimes Pat and I would go play the penny machines for a couple of hours. Usually, we kept Pat's grandson, Elijah, two days a week so his mommy could work. We started that when he was four months old. He has a little sister Erianna now so maybe we will do the same with her. Elijah liked to do sleep overs. He is very small for his age, but Erianna is a little butterball. I think helping Pat with Elijah has helped me keep so active.

I don't have much company but it is okay. I enjoy very much when we do have company. Patrick has been my right arm for twenty years at this time. He looks after me really good.

My kids wanted me to sell my mobile home estate so I sold at the worst time. It was 2011 and the economy was depressed. I had my mobile for twenty-two years. I sold it for thirty-five thousand dollars. I bought quite a bit of new furniture and enjoyed gambling with the rest. Wish now that I had invested some as now I am on a strict budget.

I was lucky in finding this nice comfortable two bedroom house. Pat and I share the rent. The house is easy to maintain and I don't have to repair anything. My mobile was a 1972 and probably the water lines are going to start leaking. It would have been my job to get them fixed. Now, if there is a problem with the house, I just call the property manager and they send someone out to fix it.

In 2011 Pat and I went to Colorado, South Dakota, and Minnesota. We went to see Sharon, my sister, in Aurora, Colorado. We then went to South Dakota to visit Mount Rushmore then to the Badlands. On to Minnesota next to visit sister Mary Ruth and Jim Artz. Good thing we did since they moved to Florida thereafter. Mary Ruth was in real bad health. Jim's health was not good either. I probably saw them for the last time as they can't come to see me or I to go there anymore.

We went to South Dakota and to my amazement, that little town of Gettysburg had changed so much. The last time I was there was in July 2003.

I can't believe I'm still able to get around as good as I do. I hate to say my bowling is bad but I still bowl Monday nights, Tuesday morning, and Thursday nights. No one ever says anything derogatory about my poor bowling but instead praise and cheer me on. I'm their inspiration to keep going. I still keep a fairly clean house but do less cooking. My fantastic son-in-law, Duane, loves to cook so about every so often, Dixie comes in from Kingman, Arizona, and brings many packets of frozen home-cooked meals and many combination of foods. I started having women friends coming over once a month to play cards.

Well, that was in 2019 before the pandemic came. We discontinued the playing for short time but are back in swing of it again. We started trading the game day to the players house. We have had our shots for Covid and all are doing well.

My son Terry came home to live with Pat and me. After forty-four years of marriage, the last twenty in misery, Terry left his wife and came to live with us. He has vowed to see that his nieces, Mary and Donna, were okay. He raised them. Their mother, Debbie, had epilepsy and was unable to care for the girls. Debbie passed away in 2018. The girls have jobs but Terry helped them out. Pat likes to travel so we have gone to see Sharon in Colorado every year. Dixie went with us in 2015. It was a surprise for Sharon. It was so neat to see how pleased both daughters were. On Saturday, we had a barbecue get together at Sharon's daughter's ranchette. Her daughter lives about five miles from her. It was such a nice day. Sharon's great granddaughter was being raised by Kathleen, her daughter, and husband Leo. My great granddaughter came out from Denver and had her nephew with her. So, I got to see two great, great grandchildren, Kloe and Kayden.

Patrick, his daughter, son-in-law, Elijah and Erianna went to Maryland to attend the wedding of his youngest brother, David. He was 56 and this was his first marriage. He wanted me to go but I said, "No." He had taken me and his family to North Carolina to a family reunion two years prior. They treated me like family. We had a very nice time there. This was my first east coast trip and my last. On August 4, 2021 at seven ten in the evening, Patrick got up from his recliner and went to the bathroom. A little while later, he came out, had a heart attack and fell to the floor. I called his daughter and the ambulance. The paramedics got him revived. They took him to Valley Hospital but couldn't save him.

I called my daughter Dixie in Battle Ground, Washington and she got a flight out. She helped me through my sorrow of losing Patrick. We had lived and shared my home for twenty-seven years. His passing would leave me living alone at age 97. So I was left to get a place to live but still be in the Las Vegas area. I called a lot of our friends and told them of Patrick's death. Julie, my friend of about twenty years, said I could live with her and care for me. She had recently lost her husband in June and she was alone. So, for me, I needed to get rid of furniture and move. All my children live out of state. Out of all the family, there is one Grandson and family still in Las Vegas. My grandson did not have a bedroom downstairs and it is too hard for me to go upstairs. So when Julie offered to take care of me, it didn't take long to make up my mind. It was to either go live with Dixie at her son's house or take up Julie's offer. My friends are in Las Vegas, so here I am, being spoiled rotten by Julie. She is so understanding and dear to me.

We go to listen to musicians at a couple of places every week. Julie signed me up for bowling on Tuesdays and Wednesdays. I can't bowl very good as I have three screws in each hip and had a quadruple heart surgery in 2007. I am still chugging along and enjoy life and try not to think about the past. Patrick wanted to live to see his grand kids graduate from high school, but his desire to not give up his cigarettes and alcohol were the rulers of his life. God bless him! Elijah is now ten years old and Erianna is six. They are going to be moving to Arizona soon and I will probably never see them again. They were like my own grandchildren.

THE JOY AND THE SORROW

Many things have been joyful in my life, especially in the later years when the children were married and giving us grandchildren. Soon it was time for Great Grand children. If I can remember, there are sixteen Grandchildren, forty-two Great grandchildren.

Not everything has been joyful. Three of my grandsons have passed away leaving a big void in families. The first Grandson to leave this world was in 2010. The second one was in 2020 and now in 2021 the third one. Four are in bad health and maybe leave this world before me. They have stead with me and David when they were little and full of not listening when scolded. I never spanked them. I never spanked my own when they were little. I played games with my children even though I was tired after a full day's work.

Life was beautiful but you have to be patient with little ones and they are a lot of fun. They all live many miles away and due to circumstances, I am living in a different and wonderful place. We go dancing and bowling. We like to listen to country music and modern entertainers. This country has many many good entertainers. I was forty before I had picked up bowling and still am bowling at 97. I won't tell you how bad my bowling is now. I don't throw many gutter balls but I have good days and bad days on the lanes. Everyone is so nice and make me feel like a queen and an inspiration to them.

I like to tease and joke with those who have the talent to tease back. So many people want to know how I accomplished reaching my age and my answer to them is "I never smoked or drank and always worked hard." I retired at the age of eighty-one and I still wish I could work. God has my life in his hands. My goal is to live to a hundred. So many joyful things still come my way. Making me a matriarch with two great, great, great grandchildren, a boy and a girl.

Oh my, I try to live by the rules of an elderly person.

JUST DIRT

*I*n 1962 when we sold our farm, we took a long across country trip throughout Montana, Idaho, then south into Oregon then back up to Washington before going down Highway 101 to Northern California. Las Vegas was the end of searching to get away from the snow and cold.

So, what did we find but warm weather and a desert area. My kids were too old to play in the desert sand but three Grandsons came and stayed a week as their mom and dad were getting settled in California. The ants were bad and sometimes the boys came in from the desert crying from ant bites.

When we moved to Las Vegas, it was small at that time. There weren't very many businesses along Boulder Highway. Only once did I have to take a bus. Being on a farm all my life made for a scary bus ride. I drove the rest of my twenty-five years on the job. There were only a couple of stop lights then. We lived in East Las Vegas. There was a drive-in movie along Boulder Highway, a ten cent store, and a pizza place. Now Boulder Highway is a very busy highway. East Las Vegas consisted of a service station, a small grocery outlet, a post office and three streets. Nothing was seen going up Boulder Highway for quite a few miles.

If I wanted to go out of town, there was a two lane highway to California; a two lane highway to the Northwest going to Reno; a two lane highway Northeast. Mesquite was along the way and you were greeted by a big cattle ranch just before getting there.

Going Northwest of Las Vegas was Mount Charleston, with a restaurant, bar, and a place to let your hair down and relax.

To the west is Death Valley which already had people settling or homesteading starting small towns and mining.

Finally, people were coming to Las Vegas and oh my, how the town isn't a town anymore but a big city. The population has grown and used up the desert that was here when we came in June 1962. Las Vegas has been my home area since then.

We moved to Palm Street in 1969. David passed in 1988 and I moved to Mabel Street in 1990 to live close to my sister. She asked me to move close to her and she was a hop-skip-and jump away which was two homes from me. During the eighteen years of living close, she would only come over to my house once. I went to her house every week. That wasn't fair, huh! There was just a lot of dirt in Las Vegas. Pretty barren at the time. I have lived in Las Vegas for many years and watched the "just dirt" turn into a big city. It is my home.

EPILOGUE

My goal is to live to a hundred. Will I make it? Sometimes I feel my age and sometimes I feel about seventy. I worked until I was eighty-one years of age and quit driving the car about five years ago. I miss not driving and don't own an automobile. I still have a driver's license but am planning to trade it in for an identification card. I became a great, great, great Grandmother in November 2018. My grandchildren, great grand children, great great grandchildren, and great great great grand children live in California. I am the matriarch of six living generations and about the seventh in the whole world. Amazing what God has planned for me. God must have something more for me yet. Only God knows. I am a proud lady.

CHERISHED THOUGHTS THROUGH EULALIA'S POETRY

A FRIEND

I once had a friend
Who came to my aid
But God took her away
Her deeds were unpaid

She adopted two children
When infants so small
And loved them dearly
Even though they were surly

Now Johnnie was tall
With hair so dark
Like the only father
He ever knew

Becky was short
With hair so light
Like her mother
Chubby and cute

The Lord took her to
Heaven In her early sixties
I miss her
I miss her

HOBBIES

What is so neat
Having something to do
Creating some things
Enjoying it too.

Whether it's sewing or painting
Now isn't that great
Or ceramics, all kinds
Pack them away in a crate.

Now writing is fine
Takes up some time
Makes you use your mind
Might even help mankind.

MY PETS

Goldie is the loving one
She curls up in my lap
And purrs and purrs
She wont be undone

Her claws come out
And kneads and kneads
Until she falls asleep
Her soul to keep

Now Fluffy is her sister
Her personality so different
Her long tail and hair
Are like a twister.

She likes to be petted
But is so skittish
She spends her time
Hidden and a might fetish.

Now we have Bob
Shines a coat of black
Owner came and got him
But he came right back.

He took over the couch
And Pat's bed too.
Eats all the food
He's no slouch.

He meows and cries
Sounds like he says "mama"
Out one door and in the other
Like I really am her mother.

MY RECIPE FOR A HEALTHY ATTITUDE

I'm sitting here
With pen in hand
And a pad

I've dressed myself
And made my bed
But,

I smile.

Thank you God
For I am able

Fixed my breakfast
Sit at the table
I can still smile.

A smile
Each and every morning
Even if the rain is pouring.

Smile.

Now the task is
What should I do?
Mop the floors
Or clean and dust
Or just

Smile.

The work can wait awhile
I'll just find something
That's fun
And sit here and

Smile.

I WISH

I wish and dream away
What is left to say
Can't make the heartache
Go far away.

My son, he seldom comes
He's not too far away
To come and say
"Mom, how are you today?"

I have four girls
Like rings and pearls
One nearby
Whose a jewel
No lie.

One so many miles from home
In poor health but doesn't complain
Needs help when she wants to roam
God help her to remain.

The oldest is a Mother, Grandmother,
And a Great Grandma
She waits on them all
Loves us all, a heart of gold.

The youngest, so jolly
A charm, like no other
She's such a joy
And never once coy.

BOARDING HOUSE

There came a day
Some time ago
Someone lost their way
Came to my door
I couldn't say no

People around make me happy
Some days they make me blue
Some days I'm a little snappy
But I'm always honest and true

Sometimes things make me sad
I feel so sorry then
Somethings make me mad
What to do and why and when

It's all my fault
My heart is so big
I'll never ever learn
Here we are

My eyes are open wide
So come on inside
But just keep on hoping
You'll find a better place to reside

I need someone around
To help me if I need
But as yet I'm abound
So don't worry or take heed

Just me

A NEW DAY

The sun comes up
With a shine so bright
So different from
The dark of night

People will scurry
To get to work
Leaving behind something
They're in such a hurry

Their worries and cares
In the back of their mind
Thinking of work
And what they will find

Will it be a nice day
Or problems galore
Sadness should someone get injured
Or more

SILENCE

Oh! The bliss
Helps you think
What am I doing, anything
I wont miss.

I sit here in my comfy chair
Think good thoughts
Even say a prayer
For I think nought

My days are numbered
This I know
For I am
Now eighty four.

Don't be silly
For life roads are hilly
Ups and downs and all around.

Everything is Silence.

SMILE

A little smile
May go a mile
To bring a new friend
Once in a while.

A smile wont break your face
Can set you on jitters
Make your heart race
Slow down, slow the pace.

Smile at a child
Whether big or small
Then comfort them
Really wont hurt at all.

A friendly smile
Can do no harm
It really is a new style
Makes one happy No alarm.

MY HOUSE

My house is but a humble home
For family and friends galore
To tell their tales and more
Wishing for happiness to come.

It's the story of my life
To give out love and caring
With very little strife
And hospitality I'm sharing.

I'm too old to send them away
Can always find some more space
For God made me this way
Not ready to take me to his place
Thank you Lord For I am happy.

WRITE ME A LETTER

Write me a letter
So neat and fine
No one could do better
Let it be one of a kind
Sweet endearing words
For my eyes to read A
nd my heart to feelings
Not silly, make it real

You may be tall
Just be on the ball
Do not fake it
Not one little bit

I walked in the sunlight
Looking for that letter
Thinking maybe it might
Make me feel better

Now isn't this something
I have all I need
Just a dreamer at heart
I'll do a good deed

LONESOME

Why be lonely
Why be sad
There are better days
So, don't be mad

Keep yourself busy
Even if playing games
Don't knock yourself dizzy
Or call anyone names

Your loneliness is you
To do whatever is needed
To keep from being blue
Use your mind unheeded

Take care of the blues
I'm sure you can
Good things come in twos
Or maybe a good man

This is really me
As I'm sure you can see
I do the best I can
Don't need a man

1924

It was January second nineteen twenty four
It was about one thirty in the morning
When my parents, who were very poor
That Dad harnessed the horses
To the bobsled so neat
But without any heat

The snow was blowing and so deep
The horses plowed on
For many miles
First going for the midwives,
Cousins Mary and Ruth

Then out again and on his way
Hoping tomorrow would be a better day
He was on his way to get old Doc Hurley
Doc Hurley was mighty and burly

I was brought into this world
No banners were unfurled
A tiny might so sweet and light
Sister Dorothy could carry me alright

Now I'm old, but not feeble
Spry as a chicken
At eighty-five years old
What a life, still very bold

Everyone who meets me
Thinks I'm so neat
I am a Halloween treat
Ho! Ho! Ho! Just me

WHAT' NEW

Many things happen
The news is on
Several fires and burns
One of life's bad turns

Drownings of tots
Unexplained mishaps
Makes one cry
And others will pry

The world's in a turmoil
Don't know which way to turn
Needs smart people
With American concern

So what's going to happen
We just have to wait
And see
And pray God help thee

FALL

The leaves are turning color
The air cools a might
Soon will be winter
On this cool cool night

Now they are falling
Like snowflakes so white
Now comes the work
To make the yard look right

Rake and rake the leaves
Before snow falls
It's such a short while
Til we can make snowballs

But fall is such a lovely time
Not too hot and not too cold
Just put on your sweater T
emperature don't really matter

THE SKY

The blue of the sky
So bright and clear
Not a cloud to be seen
No rain is near

Don't let it fool you
For it can change fast
The beautiful sky
May not last

One day the clouds came
As white as snow
With odd shapes
Hanging low
Some shaped like idols
of recognized fame

The weather predictors
They hit and miss
For it can change
Like a boa constrictor

TAKE A WALK

Take a walk down lover's lane
Or out in the pasture green
Where the cows can roam
It can be fun
On the run

There are many miles to walk
Take along a friend and talk
It's no fun to walk alone
Should you trip over a stone

Walk a fast mile
For your health
Or a slow walk
To save your energy and wealth

Do not hasten
Times not a wastin'
Or you can save the walk
Just sit down and talk

(A little advice from your mom)

SELECTION

The choices we make
Don't always help
Someone else's
Really take the cake

We struggle to make a life
To have someone or two
Change the laws
Wow what strife

Our money is short
So we try to select
Who'll help us most
What's the use to elect

But try we must
To make ends meet
And hope the officials
Feel the heat

NIGHT TIME

I should say bedtime
School kids at eight
Workers at ten
Retirees, who cares

Sleep comes early
For young and old
When the sun goes down
The same all over town

If early to bed
And early to rise
Then it's a long day
Don't take it away

NAMES

So what's in a name
Whether it be common
Or one of fame
Belongs to a person
Place or thing

Names can be short
And easy to say
Others are long
Right or wrong

Some have funny meanings
Some true feelings
Copied from older kin
Some good and some with sin

Now my name is strange
Said in many ways
Way out of range
But who cares, another day

MERRY

My days are merry
They are bright
It's up to you
To make them right

Some days you're up
Some days you're down
So smile awhile
It goes many a mile

Life can be great
It's what you make it
So close your eyes for a bit
Drive away the hate

So turn on the music
And sing and dance
And think a little
About love and romance

It won't hurt at all
But feel relieved
Be careful, don't fall
So good it will make you believe

No more simple advice
Just plain knowledge
I've done it more than twice
And it's very very nice

DAYS GONE BY

What is the best
And all of the rest
To sit in your chair
And think what is fair

Times have changed
So drastically
My life disarranged
But sometimes fantastically

Think of the days
Already gone by
Think what you may
Don't let memories die

Walk, talk, and smile
At least once in a while
It will be good for your ego
I thank God, I'm still here

A STORY

Tell me a story
So great and true
Can be many lines
Or just a few

Life can be a dream
To be told now and then
May be cheery thoughts
Make you laugh and scream

Now wouldn't that be great
If more stories were told
Make the person feel better
Happy and bold

CLOUDS

The sky is dreary and gray
The clouds are hanging low
The rain it came for a while
It's like a brand new style

The desert is dry
And needed the rain
We could use some more
Of the same
Clouds rumble like a train

Will open up and pour down rain
Make desert plants grow again
To bold so bright
Along the terrain

COME DANCE WITH ME

Come dance with me
So light and free
The band is playing
So we are staying

Waltz me around
So easy and graceful
Every step is perfect
No better can be found

Exercise the doctor says
Is good for you
As walking a mile
Brings hugs and kisses
And a smile

Our days are numbered
By the grace of God
A delightful form of mod
Each step encumbered

Teach all children
The steps are easy
Hike up the rhythm
And swing them clearly

Wasn't this fun Keep you on the run
Don't slow down Go out on the town

David McCauly and Eulalia Bartels married April 19, 1940

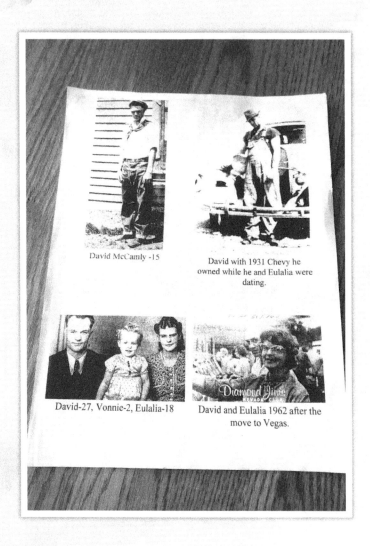

CPSIA information can be obtained
at www.ICGtesting.com
Printed in the USA
BVHW042158311022
650823BV00005B/63